Temporary INSANITY:

APPLICATION, INTERVIEW AND WORK
LESSONS TO BE LEARNED FROM THE
WORLD OF TEMPORARY STAFFING
AGENCIES AND HUMAN RESOURCES

By: Alan Balmer

Temporary INSANITY

Published by:
Intermedia Publishing Group, Inc.
P.O. Box 2825
Peoria, Arizona 85382
www.intermediapub.com

ISBN 978-0-9825942-0-9

Copyright © 2010 by Alan Balmer

Printed in the United States of America by Epic Print Solutions

TABLE OF CONTENTS

PROLOGUE:

Thanks to my wife Vickie. For over 20 plus years she has endured my idiosyncrasies, eccentricities and periodic craziness. More importantly, I would not be the man I am today without her. Here's to the hope of another 20 plus years together. As the 1987 song title from the Dirty Dancing soundtrack says…"I've had the time of my life," and furthermore the lyrics go on to say "and I owe it all to you"!!!!

Also, a big shout out goes to my two boys, Jake and Luke. I know that during the writing of this book I was deeply engrossed in the finish line of completing the book and I want to say thanks to you for understanding why Daddy wanted to get the book completed. So, thanks to my Big Man, Jake, and my Little B, Luke.

Major kudos go out to my wife and Chris Jones for being the first two to read the rough (I really mean ROUGH) draft of this book. Without their outstanding recommendations in the areas of English, grammar and writing I would be in a world of hurt. Once again, thanks you two!!!!!

Next, I want to say thanks to my other family members and friends (you know who you are) who gave me encouragement and inspiration along the way in writing this book.

Also, for every person that has ever worked for me in a staff position in a temporary/staffing agency, I want to say thanks. My professional career would not be where it is without the strong team efforts that you provided along the way. I have only been as good as those that have surrounded me and for that I say THANKS!!!!

Also, I want to thank Jon Gallo. When I was but a bean counter, Jon Gallo hired me as Controller at the organization where he was President. Since it was a small manufacturer, he also thrust upon me the mantle of Human Resources. I had no idea what to do in Human Resources, but Jon showed me the ropes as it pertains to crisis resolution, interviewing skills & investigation skills (as well as taking me to play golf and showing me how to dodge punches by crazy temporary associates).

Also, at a huge transitional point in my professional career a lady by the name of Patti Penny played an unbelievable role in my professional career by hiring me into her organization, Penmac Personnel Services. With what I would consider to be insight from God, you hired, trained, trusted, promoted and equipped me to work in the field of temporary services. I will never forget what you did for me (and my family).

Special thanks for inspiration and creative input go out to my contractor room friends at the client where I worked on-site.............

Larry Sims, President of Useless Information

Steve Perry, Vice-President of Useless Information

BB Davis, Chairwoman of the Board

Patrick Parton, Secretary of Google

Dan Close, Stealth Czar

Cheryl Chandler, Secretary of Transportation

Shay Mitchell

Mark Johnson

Chad Reid

Lastly, but most importantly, I give thanks to my Lord and Savior Jesus Christ... "He brought me out of the miry clay, He set my feet on the rock to stay, He puts a song in my soul today, A song of praise, Hallelujah."

ALAN BALMER

Introduction:
Let's Get It Started
(The Black Eyed Peas – 2004)

I have joked for many years now that one day I was going to write a book about all the stuff that happened while working in the field of Human Resources but it was always out of frustration that I made these comments. The frustration occurred for me either when I was in the middle of investigating a "situation" that involved employees or when an employee or applicant did something that was very wrong, unusual or disappointing. Regarding these investigations (or hair pulling out sessions) and/or wrong actions by employees I would make the comment to my Human Resource professional colleagues "I'm going to write a book about this." Keep in mind that my comments were seriously only a joking matter…I really had no intention of writing a book about these "situations." Then, one day, someone I worked with introduced me to the social networking phenomenon of Facebook. As I began to connect with friends on Facebook I found myself with an outlet for sharing my daily "I'm going to write a book" frustrations that occurred in the workplace. Periodically I would share with my Facebook friends funny situations that were going on. Of course, I left out the names to protect the innocent (at least they were innocent until proven guilty). These Facebook "updates" were mostly along the lines of application or interviewing faux pas that applicants had made. As I started sharing these blunders, I soon found that my Facebook friends were enjoying them and started making comments like, "Hey you should write a book." As I began thinking about the encouraging comments from my Facebook friends, it struck me that the principles behind the Facebook posts really could be of benefit to people. So, that was it. On the evening of Wednesday, September 2nd, 2009, I made the decision to start writing this book, and writing I have been doing ever since.

My whole intention in writing this book is to really, I mean REALLY, help people with making good decisions as it pertains to applying, interviewing and being an excellent, diligent worker for the business that hires them. Through the laughter, and sometimes tears that follow, please glean the truths that are present in this book. By extracting and applying the truths in this book you can become an excellent applicant, candidate and worker.

Since my Facebook posts were so instrumental in getting this book off the ground, I have included those posts in Appendix 1. After you read all the chapters in this book, you might want to peruse Appendix 1 to see how the book was inspired by the humor and frustration in the Facebook posts. I have entitled Appendix 1... "Facebook Faux Pas Frenzy"...

Oh, by the way, you will notice that each chapter is titled with a song name. You see, one of my many idiosyncrasies is that song names and lyrics have a tendency to stick in my mind and I can't seem to shake them loose from my brain. I'm not sure if this is a result of being a child and young person in the late 70's and all of the 80's, but it could be as I've noticed this tendency in other peers of mine that grew up in the 80's especially. My wife mostly, but other family members as well as friends Steve Hunt, Rev. Brett Kuchinksi, Jeff Johnson & Steve Mathis know that for some strange reason I can burst into 60's, 70's or 80's (and some early 90's) rock, pop or country songs in an instant when triggered by a word or phrase that someone utters. And, no matter where I am and regardless of the situation, I feel compelled to start singing those songs (in spite of my lack of vocal abilities). For example, one time during a teaching session my pastor and friend, Rev. Brett Kuchinksi, was presenting a lesson on controlling our emotions and I turned to my friend and fellow church member Jeff Johnson and quietly started singing "Sweet Emotion" by Aerosmith. Anyhow, I say all this to let you know that I have purposefully titled each chapter with a song title to help you remember the points I'm trying to make in this book. When you have completed reading this book my intention is that you will be able to reflect back to the chapter title index, read the chapter titles and remember the highlights of the chapter. It's what I would call a "by association" type of learning.

In the first paragraph of this chapter, I referred to "situations" that involved investigating employee's actions/comments and times when an employee or applicant did something that was very wrong, unusual or disappointing. I want to give you a quick glimpse of these types of "situations" before we move into the next chapter. The following paragraph shares this first story with you.

In the early morning hours, when one of the offices I managed was just opening, a phone call was received from a man who had been hired and placed in a temporary job/assignment at one of my company's clients. The man spoke with one of my staff members and remorsefully explained that he would not be able to make it to work that day. While this type of phone call occurs every day, numerous times, in the industry I work in, the thing that made this phone call unusual was the explanation that followed. When my staff member asked what the issue was, the employee on the other end of the phone explained that he did not want his physical situation to affect his fellow workers in the business he was working at. At this point, you are probably thinking this is a noble reason for someone to call in to work. Under most circumstances I would agree with you. However, you do not currently have all the facts in this "situation." What do you think is the type of physical "situation"/issue that the employee was calling in absent about? Is your mind filling in this missing piece of information with swine flu, Hepatitis, staph infection, a common cold or some other problem? While all of these are great guesses (but wrong), the answer is that the employee didn't want his fellow workers to catch his migraine headache. Unbelievably, the man had shared a story that just didn't line up with reality...migraine headaches are not contagious. This is just one of the hundreds and hundreds of crazy things I have experienced while working in the world of temporary or staffing agencies. As you will see throughout this book, I will share many real life examples of situations that will make you laugh. However, through the laughter that will follow as you read this book, I want to impart some principles to you that, if you will follow, will help lead you into becoming one of the best workers your organization has ever had. But, please don't limit yourself to applying the principles of this book to just your work. The principles I will share with you should guide you through many other stations in life. If you are a young person who hasn't even had their first "job," these principles will guide you in your home life as you work around the house, serving your family and friends. And, if you young person, follow these principles; it will help you as you enter your first real job and all the others that follow that. If you function in a volunteer capacity at a church, civic organization or non-profit organization, these principles will help you to strive to always give your best in every situation.

There is an old saying that goes like this..."you can't teach an old dog new tricks." I don't believe this "proverb." I believe that through the examples you will read on the pages of this book that you will see the positive impact that can be made in your life, as well as the lives of those around you. I was born in 1968 and consider myself to be young at heart even though I am, as of today, middle-aged. My observations while working have led me to a generalization. That generalization is that many in my generation and younger have nowhere near the work ethic that the generation above me or older than me has. As I have said, this is a generalization. However, my heart cries out for the youth of today because their example for work values comes from observing and following my generation and younger (as they watch their parents and others). Unfortunately, for work purposes as well as for overall life living, many times the example of the parents is not necessarily a good one. I have written this book and it applies to all people, however, if young people could grasp these concepts and principles, it will affect their lives in such a positive manner for a lifetime. My intention is to give young people some perspective on what they can do to become a great worker. However, even if you are not what you would consider a "young person," the principles in this book should help to guide you into a better understanding of what employers are looking for.

The paragraphs that follow in this introductory chapter are going to list my background. I don't list this information as a bragimonial (a self righteous, self centered, proud, attention seeking type of testimonial) but rather as some background so you can understand where the stories, principles, etc. for this book comes from. I promise only to bore you as much as necessary so you understand I really do know what I'm talking about and not just making stuff up. I am however, adept at making stuff up. My son Jake enjoys a game I made up several years ago called Fact or Fiction. Fact or Fiction is based on the premise that I try to fool him by presenting a scenario and with that scenario's information he has to decide if the scenario is Fact or Fiction. Most of the time I totally, on the fly, make something up that is Fiction but I say it with such conviction that he is not sure and as a result he feels compelled to guess. And he usually guesses Fiction and is correct. But for the purpose of this book, I have left out the Fiction and am including only Fact.

For the last 16 plus years, I have been involved one way or another in the Human Resources (in the past called Personnel) field or business. I'm not exactly sure when the name changed to Human Resources from Personnel, but I think that at some point in the 1990's it did. For those of you unfamiliar with Human Resources or Personnel, it is a department in most businesses that deals with the management of the people that work in the business or organization. Human Resource professionals get to deal with all the "fun stuff" that goes on in an organization. Here's what I mean by "fun stuff"…let's just say that an associate (once again at some point in the 1980's or 1990's depending on where you are at in the country employees were renamed associates) feels like a fellow associate has said something to them that was offensive. A later chapter in this book will deal exclusively with offenses in the workplace. At any rate, guess whose lap the allegation of this offense drops in? You guessed it, the Human Resource professional. They get the fun task of interviewing the associate making the allegation, interviewing the associate the allegation was made against, interviewing any possible witnesses, interviewing the associate's supervisors and anyone else that may or may not be involved in the situation. Sounds like fun so far doesn't it? But wait, there's more (order now and I'll throw in a set of Ginsu knives). Sorry for that digression…you'll find throughout this book that one of my eccentricities is that my mind thinks in unusual ways and I feel compelled to share it…my wife Vickie will certainly attest to this. So, back to the investigation scenario… at the end of all the investigations, the Human Resources professional gets the responsibility (er…I mean privilege) of deciding what is going to happen to the associates involved. And, I can tell you that the saying of "you can please some of the people some of the time, but not all the people all the time" is completely FACT when it comes to investigations and decision making based on the results of the investigation.

During my career in Human Resources, the first 10 were as Personnel Director or Human Resources Manager for a manufacturer. It's a funny story how I came to be in the field of Human Resources or Personnel (since I started out my career in Accounting) but we'll save that story for another time. The last 6 plus years have been involved in various capacities or roles working for Temporary Agencies or Staffing Companies. These roles include Human Resources Manager, Branch Manager, Area Manager and Onsite Program Manager. Oh, I probably need to explain what a Temporary Agency or Staffing Company is so for those of you who may not know. Temporary Agencies or Staffing Companies (also referred to sometimes as Headhunters or Placement Services) work with various businesses for the purpose of supplying the business with associates who will work for them at their place of business (but be paid by the Staffing Company). These supplied associates work on a short term temporary basis, long term temporary basis, temp to hire basis or direct hire basis. The first 10 years of my Human Resources career prepared me for the last 6 plus years working for Staffing Companies. Well, when I say prepared me, I mean like you prepare for retirement by contributing to your 401(k) plan but the stock market pulls the rug out from under you and you find yourself wondering…

will I EVER actually be able to retire (remember this is FACT not FICTION). But, the last 6 plus years of my career have been most fruitful as they are providing about 90% of the motivation for this book.

Of additional importance to understanding the work context of some of the following chapters, I need to give you a little more background about my career in the staffing/temporary industry. As I mentioned earlier, I have served in a variety of roles and responsibilities in the staffing industry but I want to explain one of them to you now. I served as the onsite program manager for several years at a client of the temporary/staffing agency I worked for. At the highest point of the program, the company I worked for had over 900 temporary associates working at this client. As the onsite program manager I had the responsibility for overseeing the day to day activities of all the temporary associates at this client. My duties, as well as the onsite staff I managed, included investigating, interviewing and intervening in "situations" that arose among associates. As you might imagine, with over 900 associates, "situations" would occur.

While being employed in the field of Human Resources, I have succeeded in making hundreds of people mad by the decisions I have made based on the correct and reasonable assessment of situations as described above. Furthermore, I have either personally been a part of or supervised staff members who have participated in hundreds and hundreds of investigations in "situations" similar to that described above. Sometimes the situations involved threats of physical harm (guns, knives, fists)....at one client the associate's favorite threat to one another was "I'll meet you at the Shell station after work." The Shell station was a gas station down the road on the corner where matters were personally, shall we say, resolved. Other situations involved physical contact on the jobsite between associates…and oh boy did the physical contact vary far and wide. Sometimes the contact was horseplay that escalated into something more, sometimes the physical contact was created by hostility and sometimes the physical contact was of a more sensual nature. Yes, it's true…you would be amazed at the physical "relations" that go on inside some businesses. Sometimes the situations involved lying, stealing, cussing, purposefully neglecting to do work…the stories are virtually endless and you will get a flavor of them throughout this book.

In addition to all the jocularity I have described above, the Human Resource professional also gets to decide who their company will hire and even more importantly I would argue, who their company DOESN'T hire. Hiring decisions are where even more "fun stuff" happens. In the chapters that follow, some will be dedicated exclusively to sharing principles with you that will help you become someone that employers will WANT to hire.

Well, I think that is enough of my background for you to absorb. I hope you enjoy the "situations" and corresponding principles from the remaining chapters in this book…I know I enjoyed writing it.

ALAN BALMER

CHAPTER 1

Don't Give Me No Lines and Keep Your Hands To Yourself (Georgia Satellites – 1986)

From my childhood to the teenage years there were two main vehicles that my family had that I remember riding in the backseat of with my sister. These vehicles were at opposite ends of the fuel efficiency spectrum. The first was a blue 1972 Chevy Impala. At 16, this became the vehicle I got to drive. This car was a very large bodied car with a 350 V8 under the hood. In high school two of my friends also had blue cars that were large…one had a blue 1977 Plymouth Sports Fury and the other had a blue 1969 Buick Electra. We used to call our cars the Big Blue Boats because they were so large. Everything in them was large…including the gas tanks because they required a LOT of gas to keep on the road for any length of time. Later on, the second car that we used a lot was a 1980 Ford Fiesta with a 4 cylinder under the hood. This car was basically a sardine can on wheels. However, despite the difference in size of the two vehicles there was one HUGE similarity between the two. Even though the Chevy Impala had a large back seat and the Ford Fiesta had a small back seat, in the middle of each back seat was an imaginary line that went right down the middle (this was a creation by my sister, Kris). And, if I took my hand (or even the tip of my finger) and crossed that imaginary line (created by my sister remember) it would provoke my sister to holler, "Mom, Alan's crossing the line!!!" At that point, I would deny this to my mother and claim that my sister was just trying to get me in trouble. But, since then I have admitted to my sister that I liked to cross the imaginary line just to provoke her. Why do I tell this story you ask? Well, there is a principle that I want to bring out, but first I have to share another story, well really a "situation"…you know I explained in the introduction that in my line of work I specialize in dealing with "situations"…well here you go…

As I was sitting at my desk at the client's workplace one day, I received a call from one of my client's supervisors stating that there was an issue that needed to be looked into. This was not unusual as most days there was some sort of issue that would come up. In actuality, we liked to joke that "situations" seemed to come in threes (similar to the theory that deaths come in threes among friends and family). After hanging up from the call, I began my way to the prearranged area of the production facility where I had agreed to meet the supervisor. After finding the supervisor, I was given a high level briefing by the supervisor. As was the practice, all "situations" are fully investigated to arrive at a conclusion. So, to begin the investigation, we called the associate in who was making the allegations and began to ask questions. After fully obtaining the associate's statement, we then called the associate to whom the allegations were being made of. To my surprise, in this situation, both stories lined up. You see, in most investigations the stories simply don't line up. The bottom line in this situation

2

was that an associate was singing around the other associate…yes that's right, SINGING. Sounds harmless enough in and of itself don't you think? The only problem was the motive behind the singing. Without getting into too much detail, the singing associate admitted to the singing but didn't admit that the motives were to annoy the other associate. However, it was the witnesses that provided the truth behind the motives. Since the singing associate wasn't willing to admit their motivation for singing, it was at this point in our conversation with the singing associate that I shared my crossing the imaginary back seat line with my sister. I explained that I had purposefully crossed the imaginary line to aggravate my sister but played it off like it was "accidental." With this modern day parable in mind, we sent the singing associate back to the production line and never again had another singing issue with the singing associate.

There are some very important principles and truths that I want to share with you that focus on motives. I hope and pray that your motives are always 100% of the time pure and righteous, but more than likely you cross the imaginary line at times with fellow associates, supervisors, subordinates or even friends, relatives and neighbors. I hope to make you think by asking you some questions, giving you some time to answer and then sharing my insight with you. Please read the following questions and then take some time to provide your own answers before proceeding to my insight.

Question #1 – What were some of the negative consequences that occurred as a result of this singing associate "situation" (think about the singing associate, the associate making the allegations, the supervisor, the witnesses and me)?

Question #2 – How do you think the singing associate was viewed going forward by his production supervisor (regardless of the fact that in the future no issues of singing for the purpose of annoyance occurred)?

Question #3 – As a temporary associate what might one of your goals be as it relates to the business you are working at and how might this situation affect that goal?

Principles/Truths from Question #1 – Negative consequences of this situation for my client included 1) Wasted time and energy for the supervisor having to sit with me on this investigation. This supervisor (along with every other supervisor) had demands on his time that makes every minute valuable. The supervisor was not able to focus on value added tasks and had to help put out this fire. I really want you to grasp the fact that businesses have a goal or mission in mind, which is to produce a product or provide a service and that "situations" like this only serve to weaken the organization because of the lack of attention that can be given during the discovery, investigation and resolution of "situations." 2) The supervisor had to scramble to find someone else to do the singing associate's job duties/processes while we were talking with the singing associate. In addition, when we interviewed the associate making the allegation as well as the witnesses we had to find someone to do their job duties/processes while we were talking to them. 3) My time, even though investigating and resolving issues is part of my job, was not able to be spent on other value added tasks for my client and the temporary agency I worked for.

Principles/Truths from Question #2 – The singing associate was viewed going forward as a trouble maker, a poor team player and a morale breaker. Anytime the singing associate did something, his motives were questioned by management. Rather than being an associate that could be trusted to do the right thing, a cloud of suspicion always encompassed the singing associate.

Principle/Truth from Question #3 – As a temporary associate, besides getting paid for working, a major goal of the temporary associate is usually to work hard to put yourself in a position to get hired directly by the company thereby increasing the likelihood that your pay will become higher and your benefits will increase. The singing associate could have severely hurt his chances of achieving the ultimate goal of being hired by my client.

The moral of this chapter is that in all your relationships at work (with your fellow workers, your supervisor or subordinates) you need to be a good team player. Trouble makers, poor team players and morale breakers are purposefully weeded out by employers… and rightfully so. This is not the only application, however. I would encourage each of you that in every relationship you have in life to be a good team player. If you are on a sports team, don't hurt the cohesiveness of the team by saying or doing inappropriate things. You will only serve to decrease the overall effectiveness of the team. If you are a volunteer at a church, civic organization or non-profit organization, don't cause waves or create tension or friction in the organization. You too, even if you aren't being paid for your services, will probably be purposefully weeded out by those in authority.

I've mentioned several of my personal insights so far…the first was that sometimes my mind thinks in unusual ways and the second was that songs and song lyrics are burned in my brain and they frequently find a way out through my vocal cords. The third insight I want to share with you is that I know beyond a shadow of a doubt that regardless of your CURRENT belief system that the Bible holds truths in it that if applied will DEFINITELY help you improve your effectiveness; not just in the workplace but in all your relationships. Therefore, I will periodically (not every chapter) be sharing some Scripture for you to reflect on. So...here goes...the first Scripture I want you to reflect on is:

"But the fruit of the Spirit is love, joy, peace, patience, kindness, goodness, faithfulness, gentleness and self-control. Against such things there is no law." (Gal.5:22-23, New International Version)

If you can cultivate this fruit in your life as it pertains to work, school, volunteerism, family and friends; you will be a great team player that doesn't feel the need to cross the imaginary backseat line in any of your relationships and will be a team member that other team members feel can be trusted. I challenge you to reflect on these "fruits" and with God's help try to develop them in your life.

The last thought I want to leave you with in this chapter is with regard to the parable of the "Shrewd Manager" in Luke 16:1-15. With regard to wealth and the management of other's wealth, verse 10 says... "Whoever can be trusted with very little can also be trusted with much, and whoever is dishonest with very little will also be dishonest with much."

I know that this passage is talking about money and I don't want to pull it out of context, but I believe that it helps to illustrate how much we need to be able to be trusted in the workplace with regard to what we say, what we do, what our motives are, and what our intentions are etc. I believe that if your employer knows, because you have proven it, that you can be trusted with the "little" things that you will be rewarded with "larger" things later. In Matthew 25:29 we are supplied with an illustration that shows how important it is to prove yourself faithful/trustworthy in all you do… "For everyone who has will be given more, and he will have an abundance. Whoever does not have, even what he has will be taken from him." In this passage, once again there is a principle as it pertains to the management of money. However, when people receive an increase in responsibility generally it is accompanied by an increase in compensation. On this point, I speak from personal experience and firsthand knowledge from those that have worked for me or around me. This is not just a theory. As you prove yourself faithful in little, you will be given opportunities to do more and generally as a result you will be blessed and rewarded.

Bottom line for this chapter…I encourage each of you to stop crossing the work and/or relationship imaginary backseat lines with anyone you are purposefully trying to annoy.

Application/reflection questions:

1. Who have you been crossing the imaginary backseat line with?

2. What steps do you need to take to make things right with that person or persons?

3. What steps are you going to take to make sure you don't cross the imaginary backseat line in the future?

4. Practically, how will you try to develop the fruit of the Spirit in your life in order to be a trusted employee, friend, family member, team member etc. in order to show that you are in fact faithful with little things in anticipation that larger or greater things will come?

CHAPTER 2
Ooooh That Smell, Can't You Smell That Smell
(Lynyrd Skynyrd – 1977)

Okay…so I am not an environmentalist by any means…even if my wife and I do own two very fuel efficient cars. The reason for their purchase is primarily due to my frugal ways (cheap if you ask my wife Vickie). See, the vehicles we purchased cost less money than other larger vehicles and they use less gas…thereby saving us money. And wouldn't you know it that one of these fuel efficient cars was purchased about a month before the Cash for Clunkers program was announced (Murphy's Law). Even though I'm not an environmentalist, it is frustrating how much Lysol the branch offices I have managed have had to go through (ozone damage and all) as a result of Stinky Petes and Smelly Sallys coming in to apply for jobs.

In my line of work, I don't think I have experienced much more frustration than having an applicant come in who has the Pepe' Le Pew syndrome. In addition, there are people who come in to apply that either smell like urine or other bodily excretions. While

I certainly don't want to judge anyone and their personal life, I and my staff in the temporary services industry do have a responsibility to provide our business clients with associates who are not going to cause aggravation, frustration and turmoil. Therefore, if you come into a temporary agency (or any business for that matter) to apply for work please, please, please make sure you have bathed, deodorized yourself, brushed your teeth etc…just plain old good personal hygiene. If you come in like a Stinky Pete or a Smelly Sally you will not get hired by me because I'm not going to send you to a client knowing that I'll have a high probability (even with me counseling you on it beforehand) of having to converse with you about it again.

Keep in mind that, in many cases, the clients that staffing agencies supply are using temporaries for screening. You may have heard the phrase before with regard to temporary services and temporaries "try em before you buy em." This is true in a lot of cases. If a client doesn't think you are going to be a good fit for their organization, they will just call the staffing agency and say something to the effect of "I don't want Stinky Pete back tomorrow, please send me a replacement." It may seem cold and cruel at times but the clients we serve have to make decisions about what is best for them.

Now, sometimes people get hired and, due to life issues, personal hygiene may become a problem for them when it was not a problem when they applied for work. On more than one occasion, I or one of my staff has had to have the awkward conversation with an associate that we placed in an assignment at a client after a client representative called and shared with us that there were personal hygiene issues. I have heard of Human Resource professionals putting together little care packages with soap, deodorant, toothpaste, feminine hygiene products, toothbrushes, combs as well as other items and giving them to "offensive to the nasal passage associates." This can be a creative way to deal with the situation. But, make no mistake about it; someone in a management role will have to deal with this situation because fellow associates around the "offending party" will create enough noise that it will have to be resolved.

Now, I need to speak to those of you who have never yourself had personal hygiene issues but know what I'm talking about in terms of Stinky Petes or Smelly Sallys. First, let me state that the comments I have made in this chapter are not meant to be demeaning to those that have issues with personal hygiene. However, I do have to make prudent business decisions as a Human Resources professional and these decisions can sometimes seem a little hard hearted. I want to encourage those of you that wrestle with how to deal with other people who struggle with personal hygiene issues to consider Scripture again. As I mentioned in the previous chapter, Scripture will give you a perspective that needs to be considered and followed. For this chapter I want you to look at Luke 6.31 which in the New International Version says, "Do to others as you would have them do to you."

Some of you may be familiar with this Scripture. This is the proverbial "Golden Rule." I encourage each of you to reflect on people that you either have not treated well or are currently not treating well. Think about if it was you that was struggling with personal hygiene issues…how would you want to be notified of the situation…in what type of way…in what tone of voice…in what setting…in what audience. Keep in mind that there are many ways to get across the same message.

Application/reflection questions:

1. If personal hygiene is an issue for you, what steps do you need to take to make sure that you present yourself in a non-offensive way when applying, interviewing or working on the job?

2. If personal hygiene is not an issue for you, do you need to change your mindset towards those that you have or will come in contact with who struggle with personal hygiene?

3. Who have you not been treating like you would like to be treated?

4. What steps do you need to take to make things right with that person or persons?

5. What steps are you going to take to make sure you don't interact with people harshly, rudely, with cynicism, with meanness (etc. etc. etc.) in the future?

CHAPTER 3
Your Cheatin' Heart…Will Tell On You (Hank Williams Sr. – 1952)

For most temporary associates, the length of assignment at the client companies we serve is generally short term (although this is not always the case). I have had clients that utilized the temporary agency as the constant, ongoing employer of record with no intention of ever hiring the temporaries full time. (Please stay with me in this chapter…I am going someplace with the boring details of this first paragraph.) Keep in mind that at the employer I am referencing there were very good benefits provided through the temporary agency specifically for this client company and also the pay rate was very competitive with the overall local market. And, due to the long term nature of the assignments, after meeting all the criteria (including total hours worked in at least a twelve month period) the associates were eligible for Family Medical Leave Act (FMLA) that provided up to twelve weeks of unpaid leave for certain medical situations. This is not the norm with most associates of temporary agencies. Because these associates are short term they don't ever get to the point where they meet the requirements to be eligible for FMLA.

As a result, at one other client I served, we had a policy that (in the absence of qualifying for FMLA during the first year) if an associate had a doctor's excuse for five business days it would not be counted negatively against them as far as the absence policy was concerned.

This five day doctor's excuse policy was something that helped many associates retain their assignment/job at this client, but for others, as you will see, it became "the straw that broke the camel's back" for some associates. You'll understand more as you read on. To illustrate this let me share some "situations" with you.

On many occasions we had associates at this client that would call in and say they were sick and had obtained a doctor's excuse. These associates identified what day(s) they would be absent and what date they were scheduled to return to work. Our telephone instructions to the associate would be to make sure and bring the original doctor's excuse with them on their day of return and report directly to the onsite medical provider at the client company the day of their return in order to obtain clearance to report back to the production floor. However, in more instances than I would like to recount, the associate returned with a doctor's excuse that appeared to either myself, my onsite staff or the onsite medical provider to be somewhat odd, strange or falsified. Here are some of the problems we found...

1. Dates that appeared to be changed on the doctor's excuse. You would be amazed to learn how angry medical providers are to find out that doctor's excuses have been tampered with. (This is far and away the most frequent situation that came up.)

2. We had men turn in doctor's excuses from OB/GYN offices. For those of you not familiar OB/GYN doctors, those are doctors that specialize in female issues.

3. We had men and women turn in doctor's excuses from pediatrician's offices stating that they were personally treated (and not a child). Keep in mind that pediatricians are doctors for children, not adults.

4. We had documents that appeared to be copied and then cut and pasted together.

5. We had documents that were hand written with such poor grammar and language that it was obvious a medical professional had not written them.

In all of these type "situations" listed above, either we or the onsite medical provider would contact the doctor's office (or other medical provider) that the excuse/return to work authorization came from in order to obtain verification regarding the authenticity of the documentation. In most of these cases it was found that the associate had falsified the doctor excuse.

I can't tell you how bad this looks to an employer or prospective employer that you were dishonest, cheated or were fraudulent (however you want to state it). First of all, if I as the current employer find this out, I am going to terminate your employment immediately with no chance of rehire. Second, who is going to want to hire someone that is known and proven as a lying, cheating fraud? No one is going to want to hire you...that is who. Be sure… your cheatin' heart will tell on you.

One of my staff members recently shared a "situation " with me of how she had an applicant in the past that appeared to meet all the qualifications necessary…work experience, work history, interviewed well and tested well but the next hurdle to clear became a hurdle that the applicant tripped over. You see, when a staffing agency (or other business for that matter) decides that they would like to hire someone, one of the final hurdles to clear is that of taking a drug test. At this particular staffing agency, we did drug tests by having the applicant provide a urine specimen in the office and used a drug test kit on the urine sample. Well, when this applicant took the drug test it came out positive; for those of you not familiar with the lingo of drug tests…positive is NOT a good thing. Positive means that you tested positive for a drug. In this case it was THC (or marijuana). Upon informing the applicant that they tested positive, without missing a beat the applicant said "I'm gonna kill that friend of mine, he gave me pee that had marijuana it." That's right, he had brought someone else's urine in to be tested because the applicant knew that they could not pass the drug test. You see, some applicants that know that they can't pass a drug test (but want a job) go to extreme measures to try and sneak in a urine sample from someone else (I'm not going to dive into the details of how they try to sneak them in….you can think creatively on your own). Anyhow…be sure…your cheatin' heart will tell on you.

Additionally, I have had several cases where associates have lost their job and had legal action taken against them due to the filing of a falsified worker's compensation medical claim. You would be amazed at the stories that were creatively fabricated to try and get an employer to pay for medical expenses that were not at all work related. Additionally, I am always amazed at how these associates cheatin' hearts tell on them. Sometimes we discover falsified claims based on conflicting information that associates provide on accident investigation forms, sometimes the information comes from the associate's colleagues that know inside information, sometimes information comes from people that know them outside of work and sometimes it comes when you see them walking around in the Wal-Mart with no signs of injury when they claim to be in excruciating pain when they come see you in the office or when they go to their doctor's appointment. Regardless, their cheatin' heart finds them out.

In the Old Testament writings of Moses, we find a particularly interesting account of the Israelites as they were about to cross the Jordan River into their Promised Land (a wonderful land that the Bible proclaims flowed with milk and honey). However, some of the Israelites wanted to stay on the east side of the Jordan and settle in that land. This ultimately was deemed acceptable by Moses under one condition. That condition was that the fighting men of the tribes who wanted to settle east of the Jordan go with the other tribes across the Jordan River to obtain/settle/conquer ALL the land that God had promised the Israelites. At the end of Moses' instructions to the tribes that wanted to settle on the east side of the Jordan he gave them the bottom line as I like to call it. The bottom line is found in Numbers 32:23 and the NIV Bible records it as follows…that which is in parentheses is added by me. "But if you fail to do this (help your fellow countrymen from other tribes obtain/settle/conquer ALL the land), you will be sinning against the LORD; and you may be sure that your sin will find you out."

I want you to understand that dishonesty, cheating and fraud are sins and they will be found out. All the examples I have shared in this chapter deal with some form or another of cheating…the person who tried to use someone else's urine, the people who changed the dates on the doctor's excuse and the people who filed false workers compensation injury claims. Let me show you further Biblical documentation of how serious God views cheating...look at Proverbs 11:1 from the NIV Bible:

"The LORD abhors dishonest scales, but accurate weights are his delight."

I want you to understand that when this was written, so much depended on weights and measures for commerce, barter and compensation. If someone had dishonest scales they were cheating other people. What does Proverbs 11:1 say about cheating? That's right...that the Lord "abhors" it. Abhor is not a word we use a lot in our culture but the original meaning behind this word is abomination, disgusting, wickedness, and unethical. I can tell you that God is not the only one who views cheating in this light, but temporary/staffing agencies as well as any other business view it in this light also. The consequences in the business world are severe for you when you are found to be dishonest, cheating or fraudulent. The consequences involve termination and prosecution just to name a few. I implore you to be honest, forthright, fair and trustworthy in all your dealings.

Application/reflection questions:

1. What past or current situations has this chapter prompted you to recall where you either have been or are currently being dishonest, cheating or fraudulent with your current or previous employers?

2. What steps do you need to take to make things right with those employers?

3. What steps are you going to take to make sure you aren't dishonest, cheating or fraudulent in the future?

ALAN BALMER

CHAPTER 4
Where Are You Now? (Synch – 1986)

Most employers have a policy that pertains to associates who just stop showing up for work. The policy usually outlines how long someone can be a "no call no show" before their assignment or job is ended for job abandonment. Yes, that's right, it is viewed as job abandonment which is you quitting without notice rather than you being terminated by your employer. At one of my clients, in a three year period, we had 277 associates who were no call no shows for three days straight (this was the policy adopted for this company). At this particular client, either myself or one of my staff members would attempt to contact the associate who was a no call no show and guess what, big surprise, the majority of the time we were unable to get anyone to answer the phone at the numbers we had listed. Many times, due to the invention of Caller ID I believe, people would not answer their phone when they saw it was a call from either the temporary agency or the client company that we called from. However, I did utilize a trick that sometimes worked

21

in making contact with people. The trick was that I would call from my business cell phone and not leave a message...then just hang up. You would be surprised how many times someone would call back (almost immediately) saying.... "Yeah, I just missed a call from this number." What was running through my mind at that point was....Oh yeah, and you just "missed" a call from the temporary agency or client company that I just tried to call you from also. Of course, I didn't say that to them...I was just thinking it (along with HMMMMMM this would make great material for a book someday). Remember, it was in "situations" like this that the joke of me writing a book would be vocalized to my Human Resource Professional colleagues.

The whole point is that there are tremendous consequences for you as the associate when you just stop showing up for work and don't bother to tell anyone...consider the following consequences of you abandoning your job.

Consequence number 1 - In the future, after you are separated (ended assignment or terminated job) for being a "no call no show," you will probably apply for a job somewhere else and due to the request on the prospective employer's application, you will be required to provide a full, complete and accurate work history which will include information about your work history at the business where you were a "no call no show." What do you think will happen when the business you are applying at sees on your application that you just stopped showing up for work? Remember...you are required to provide a full, complete and accurate work history including why you are no longer at that employer. Why would an employer want to go any further with you (interview, screening, processing, or testing for employment) when they see on your application that you just stopped showing up for work at a previous employer? You need to know that employers are looking for applicants who will be at work every day, on time, working the entire shift in order to prevent interruptions from occurring in the production and distribution of goods and/or in the providing of services. If you have not proven yourself faithful in the past then other employers are not going to want to take a chance on you.

Consequence number 2 - Let's just say "hypothetically" that you decide to not give the full, complete and accurate reason on a business employment application with regard to why you are no longer at a previous employer. Okay, so this is really not a hypothetical issue…this really does happen. Back to the point…WHEN this happens do you think that the employer that had you complete the application is going to fully rely on your representation about what happened at previous employers? Well, some will, but most likely the business is going to start making what are called "reference checks." This means that someone in the business (or someone that the business contracts with) will call your previous employers to find out what happened from that company's perspective. HMMMMMMM…How's that gonna work for you when the company you are applying to finds out that you either lied or didn't fully disclose the truth…however you want to wordsmith it?

Consequence number 3 – Let's just say that in order to prevent Consequence number 1 and Consequence number 2 you decide to take what's behind door number 3. Behind door number 3 you find a potential way to get around suffering the result of Consequence number 1 and Consequence number 2. The potential way to avoid the negative consequences, in your mind, is to just simply leave off the business employment application that you ever even worked at the employer where you abandoned your job as a no call no show. Well, I hate to blow a hole in your door number 3 revelation, but one of the biggest things that employers look for on applications are gaps in employment. You can be assured that you will get questioned during an interview by prospective employers about gaps in employment and now your boat will be full of holes again and you are sunk. Also, no need to try and smooth the application over by providing false dates on the application...that will be caught in the "reference checks" to previous employers (see Consequence number 2 above).

Consequence number 4 – As if the consequences listed above aren't enough...the dim prospect of getting another job...there is another consequence. Although I am not a lawyer (the next chapter will deal with the use of that word) and I will not provide legal advice, I can share with you from my experience what has happened to employees who abandoned their job by being a no call no show. In some cases, associates who have abandoned their job have decided that they would just collect unemployment...as if it is their own personal decision about the award of unemployment benefits. The truth is that most states have a department, group or branch that deals almost exclusively with the awarding of unemployment benefits. These state departments, groups or branches are the ones who make the determination about who gets unemployment benefits and who does not. And, from the experience I have had in 2 of the 50 states, the associate almost always does not get awarded unemployment benefits when they abandon their job as a result of being a no call no show. I can't count the number of times either I or a staff member has had to respond to unemployment department requests for information on ex-associates that were a "no call no show." In addition, I have had to participate in unemployment hearings by telephone for this very reason. On many an occasion after the unemployment office denies their benefits, the denied ex-associate will call me and question (although question is kind of light description…the majority of the time it is complaining, hollering, cussing etc…you get the picture), why I worked so hard to deny their benefits at the hearing. HELLO…why would I want to let you have something that you aren't entitled to (unemployment is not like the 1985 song by Dire Straits titled "Money For Nothing"). I am charged by my employer to manage well what I have been entrusted with (refer back to Chapter 1…being faithful with small and large things). Part of that responsibility is managing unemployment claims. See, in the states where I have operated, unemployment insurance is something that the employer has to pay for, not the associate. There has been a misconception among some associates and ex-associates that THEY, and not their employer or ex-employer, are paying into the unemployment fund.

Alright, so to wrap up this chapter, I just want to emphasize the importance of leaving a job well. There are ways to leave a company on good terms, but just not showing up for work or not calling in is not a good option. **Always, always, always** stay in communication with your supervisor AND your Human Resources department. Also, if you are a temporary or will be one in the future, it is NOT enough to only tell someone at just the client company/business where you are working or just the temporary agency. You MUST tell someone at both the client company and the temporary agency…and it would be wise of you to do it in writing so there is a record of it for the future. And, you need to abide by the notice requirements that your employer has…some have a one week notice requirement, some have a two week notice requirement…in order to leave on good terms. Please, please, please follow this insight and you will make yourself more valuable in the eyes of employers. Don't make your supervisor, Human Resources department or anyone else at your employer have to question "Where Are You Now?"

Application/reflection questions:

1. Have you personally (or through the example of friends, family members, neighbors or co-workers) experienced the negative consequences of being a "no call no show"?

2. What steps do you need to take to make sure you don't fail to remember the importance of calling in when you will be absent?

3. Based on the "negative consequences" section of this chapter, do you realize how important it is to leave your current and/ or future jobs on good terms? What will you do if a company offers you a job and says you HAVE to report immediately and not give your current employer notice of your intent to quit?

ALAN BALMER

CHAPTER 5

Talk To My Lawyer (Chuck Brodsky - 1996) or Better Get A Lawyer (The Cruel Sea – 1995)

As I said in the introduction, I have made hundreds of associates and applicants mad over the decisions I have made with regard to "situation" resolution, but also with regard to decisions about which applicants I would NOT hire. I want you to keep in mind that my company, or any other business for that matter, does not have an obligation or responsibility to hire any and everyone that applies. Temporary agencies and the client businesses that we serve are not social organizations or not-for-profit governmental agencies. Temporary agencies and the client businesses that we serve are for profit organizations that have to make decisions about applicants based on the information that is available from applications, interviews, references, testing etc. The decisions that we make about applicants are for the benefit of our business or organization. There are times that we pass over "good" applicants and select an applicant that is "great." However, "bad" applicants will get passed over routinely. I always try to let applicants know why I won't hire them. This is my personal conviction because I want the applicant to have a chance to take the information and improve in future application or interview opportunities. However, there is no obligation on my part or any other Human Resource professional to give you any or all the reasons why an applicant is not being hired. And, in many cases Human Resources professionals will not give you that information.

With the previous chapter in mind, I can't tell you the number of times the big "L" word has been thrown at me. Any guesses as to what "L" word I'm talking about? No, it's not "loser" with the big "L" on the forehead. Well, by the title of the chapter, you may have guessed "Lawyer." That's right folks….the threat of "calling a lawyer" has been used on me or my staff members countless times.

Let me tell you the words lawyer, attorney, legal counsel etc. don't scare me. The first, and most important reason, is because I trust my own judgment and decision making skills (this is not a boastful, proud or arrogant statement). The second reason is because I have come to learn that in the course of business there will be times when lawyers have to get involved and when they do I just simply take it all in stride. It is just a normal course of action in some "situations" to have lawyers get involved. However, I am not scared (and most Human Resource professionals are not either) when you throw it out there that you are going to call a lawyer. Can I tell you that for the last 6 plus years I have developed two responses that I use when someone tells me they are going to get a lawyer. I know that through the course of this book you have seen that I have developed some cynicism and sarcasm (the other day I made a comment and my sister replied that I was being "edgy"…I like that word…"edgy"). The two responses to lawyer threats that

I am going to share with you below will show you a little bit more of my periodic "edgy" side.

Response #1 to people that say they are going to get a lawyer – "Do you know of any good lawyers? Because, I could give you the names of some if you don't have one."

Response #2 to people that say they are going to get a lawyer – "I really look forward to talking to your lawyer."

It just depends on what mood strikes me that determines the response I use. Let me just give you some real life "situations" where I have heard the "L" word thrown around.

1.   At the staffing agency where I currently work, we changed our process to not printing check stubs for associates to pick up at our branch offices. The check stubs are now available online and the associates have their username and password that will allow them to go to our website to view and/or print them. One day an associate was highly agitated that we had switched to this policy and demanded that we either print the check stubs off for him or that we compensate him for the time that it took him to do it himself. After overhearing that he was giving a staff member grief for this I intervened and explained the policy multiple times along with how he could get the information online. After not being able to satisfy this associate he said to me, "Well, I guess you'll be hearing from my lawyer." To which I used one of my two responses above. So far, I haven't heard from his lawyer.

2. Recently, I had an aggravated applicant meet with me for the purpose of trying to determine why we had not hired her (as well as "some people" she knew). At the end of the conversation I heard the famous "L" line.

3. Countless times I or one of my staff members has had to end the assignment of an associate at one of our clients that we serve. Although the circumstances are too numerous to list, I have taken phone calls from the ended associates and the outcome was the famous "L" line. At one point in my career, there was an attorney sitting in the general area where I sat. She always got a chuckle after overhearing one of these conversations I was having on the phone.

The point is that idle threats are useless and it usually doesn't make Human Resource professionals fret, become scared or worrisome. And, by you throwing that idle threat out there, it will not change the decision that has been made. Oh...by the way... threatening to make an Equal Employment Opportunity Commission (EEOC) claim doesn't invoke feelings of fright either. I've heard the threat of contacting the EEOC numerous times as well. Most Human Resource professionals at one time or another have to deal with lawyers, governmental agencies etc. and it is routine. In fact, one time I had to take an entire week away from my normal work responsibilities and sit through a trial (as a witness) because of a "situation" that an ex-associate made an allegation over. Ultimately, we defended the case successfully and were vindicated. However, it sure did waste a lot of people's time and money. To get on a political soapbox, I would like to see reform in the legal system that penalizes the plaintiff or claimant for bringing cases that are found to be frivolous after trial. I think they should have to pay the defendant's legal fees, wages and lost opportunity costs of cases that are lost. I think this would also limit the number of cases that some lawyers would take.

In Psalm 10, the writer describes the "wicked man," and verse 7 of the 10th Psalm says,

"His mouth is full of curses and lies and threats; trouble and evil are under his tongue."

I want to encourage you to be a person that never utters curses, lies or threats. Don't be a "wicked" person according to this Biblical passage. I can assure you that as Human Resource professionals we want nothing to do with people that curse, lie and make threats. Put yourself in a position to be a trusted employee by refraining from these activities.

Application/reflection questions:

1. Who have you been cursing at/about, lying to and threatening? (This is not just a work question....consider all your relationships.)

2. What steps do you need to take to make things right with that person or persons?

3. What steps are you going to take to make sure you don't engage in these types of verbal assaults in the future?

CHAPTER 6
My Mama Said (ABBA - 1974) or Mama Told Me (Three Dog Night - 1970)

I have been the most embarrassed for those applicants that are brought in…well really drug in…by their mamas to apply for a job. The conversation usually plays out like this:

Temporary Agency Front Desk Person: "Welcome to XYZ Staffing Service (Temporary Agency). How can we help you today?"

Applicant's Mama: "This is my son, Bobby, and he needs a job so he can get out of my house."

Temporary Agency Front Desk Person (to Bobby…not Mama): "Bobby, is it true you want to apply for employment today?"

Applicant's Mama: "That's right he wants a job!!"

Temporary Agency Front Desk Person (to Mama): "Ma'am since you say Bobby needs a job and he will be applying I really need to speak to him and not you."

Applicant's Mama: "Just tell me what I got to do to get Bobby a job!!"

And, the conversation deteriorates further from there but you get the general picture by now I'm sure. The conversation can vary somewhat from time to time but the essence of it is usually the same and the overbearing Mama, thinking she is going to help "Bobby" get a job generally ends up hurting "Bobby's" chances of gaining employment. See, the premise is that the temporary agency (and the businesses they serve) don't care how much Mama wants you to have a job. We are interested in "Bobby's" desire to be employed...not Mama's. What I have observed is that generally Bobby won't have the motivation to work hard, be at work on time, and work the entire shift etc., etc., etc. so why would I want to hire Bobby? Bottom line...don't come to apply and give us the line "Mama said I got to get a job"...it won't be in your best interest to reveal that inside information.

Also, consider that it isn't always Mama that brings someone in. I've seen wives bring in their husbands; grandparents bring in their grandchildren etc. The point is DON'T DO IT!!! Someone 18 years of age or older should be able to take personal responsibility and seek employment on their own. Does this mean that Mama or other family members or friends should not be advising them from behind the scenes? Not at all, but Mama doesn't need to come with "Bobby" to apply.

Some additional things to consider…when you (I say "you") come to apply, don't bring your entire family or friends with you. We don't want to have a lobby full of people talking to each other, babies crying, people talking on cell phones & generally creating an environment that is not conducive to interviewing, answering phones etc. (all the normal business things that go on in a temporary agency). Please note that children should not be brought with you when you apply. The temporary agency is not like the pediatrician's office that my sons go to. Unlike our pediatrician's office, temporary agencies don't have an Xbox, a toy box full of toys or a room dedicated to securing your children. It's not that we don't like children, it's just that they are not conducive to the normal business environment.

Let me leave with you some selected passages of Scripture as found in the Wisdom Literature of the Bible. These are found in the Biblical book of Proverbs and are quoted from the NIV.

The first three passages are proverbs of Solomon as found in Proverbs 10.

"A wise son brings joy to his father,

but a foolish son grief to his mother." (10:1)

"Lazy hands make a man poor,

but diligent hands bring wealth." (10:4)

"He who gathers crops in summer is a wise son,

but he who sleeps during harvest is a disgraceful son." (10:5)

Proverbs 13:4

"The sluggard craves and gets nothing,

but the desires of the diligent are fully satisfied."

Proverbs 14:23

"All hard work brings a profit,

but mere talk leads only to poverty."

Take a moment to reflect back on these five passages of Scripture. As you do, answer the following questions:

1.   What are some of the positive outcomes for those that are wise, hardworking and diligent?

2.   What are some of the negative outcomes for those that are foolish, lazy, mere talkers and sluggards?

Application/reflection questions:

1. After reflecting on the "outcomes" in the five passages in Proverbs, do you find yourself to be wise, hardworking and diligent, or foolish, lazy, a mere talker and a sluggard? (The outcomes should give you insight into this.)

2. If you now realize that you are in the foolish, lazy, mere talking sluggard category, how will you shake yourself into becoming wise, hardworking and diligent?

3. Do you find yourself identifying more with Mama, Bobby or neither?

4. If you find yourself identifying more with Mama, what steps do you need to take to release your child into independence?

5. If you find yourself identifying more with Bobby, what steps do you need to take to move from riding Mama's coat tails into independence?

ALAN BALMER

CHAPTER 7

Itsy Bitsy Teeny Weeny Yellow Polka Dot Bikini
(Brian Hyland - 1960)

I've never been what you would consider to be a "suit and tie" guy. During the first two and a half years of my professional career I worked in a Certified Public Accounting (CPA) firm in Kansas City, Missouri and was required to wear a suit and tie every day. Let's just say I despised wearing a suit and tie. When I left the CPA firm I went to work for a manufacturer and got to wear dress pants and a nice pull over or button up shirt…and I LOVED it. From that point on, much to my wife's displeasure, the wearing of a suit and tie gradually decreased to the point where I only wear ties at funerals (and not all funerals) and don't even wear a tie, blazer or suit jacket when I have the occasion to speak at church. At this point in my life I wear dress pants and a nice pull over or button up every day (including to church) and I love it. Before I presented my main point in this chapter I wanted to make sure you understood that I'm not a legalistic "dress up" suit and tie guy.

I recently had the privilege of sharing interview/application tips (as well as tips about how to be a good employee or associate) at a job fair that a local church was conducting for the community. In the job fair there were two staffing/temporary agencies slated to speak of which I was scheduled first. Part of what I had predetermined to talk about was the type of dress that was inappropriate for applicants to wear when coming to the office to complete paperwork and an interview (please note that the following tips are not just for applicants to staffing/temporary agencies but pertain to any business you might be applying at). At the job fair I was sharing that it is not appropriate to wear certain types of clothing for applying and interviewing. Also, remember that this book is based on FACT (not FICTION) and I'm not making up the following. The main emphasis of my clothing comments at the job fair speech was that women should not wear the following: spandex, sports bras, halter tops etc. to apply or interview in. I shared the fact that regardless of the woman's physique it is not appropriate to show skin in an interview especially if the woman has, shall we say, excess weight that rolls over, out and beyond the spandex, sports bras, halter tops etc. Of course, the comment got a good laugh from the job fair attendees. But, what owned me was what my colleague from the other staffing/temporary agency said about my comments. The colleague said that they have a saying for "larger" women that come in wearing spandex, sports bras, halter tops etc. My colleague told me that they call that "coming in looking like a busted can of biscuits"… I'm sorry but I forgot to tell you to turn off your mental visual images prior to the statement…my apologies. The "busted can of biscuits" comment entertained me so much that during the following weekend I posted my very first "job related" comment on Facebook and it was with regard to "coming in looking like a busted can of biscuits." This Facebook post or comment set the wheels in motion for future interview/application tips that were posted on Facebook and ultimately helped me to launch into the writing of this book with the encouragement of my Facebook friends and family.

The entire point to this chapter is that there are certain items of clothing that most staffing/temporary agencies as well as businesses don't appreciate you wearing to apply in, interview in or wear to work every day. I have included below a list of items of clothing you should not wear to apply in, interview in or to work in.

1.   Ladies, as I've already mentioned, don't wear spandex, sports bras or halter tops to apply, interview, or work in. Also, please include in this category, no swimsuits. Let's keep in mind that, although in my experience the staffing/temporary world is dominated by women, men are visually oriented and for those of us men in the staffing/temporary world we certainly don't need to focus on your body or be distracted during the interview.

2.   Guys, wife beater undershirts by themselves are not appropriate. The ladies that work in the staffing/ temporary agency don't want to see your underarm hair while they are interviewing you. If you are going to wear a wife beater undershirt make sure you have a nice pullover or button up shirt covering it.

3.   Guys, also, I am aware that in certain cultures in our society it is acceptable, approved and the norm to wear your jeans down…either on or below your butt showing your underwear (called slacking). However, it is NOT appropriate to slack when you come to apply

and interview. Regardless of the staffing/temporary agency's employees being men or women, no one wants to see your underwear. And, the client businesses that we serve don't want associates working for them that are going to be showing their underwear.

4. Guys and gals, I would ALWAYS rather see an applicant wear a nice pullover or button up shirt, but if you must wear a T-shirt then for the love of peace don't wear something that has nasty, offensive, dirty or racial comments or pictures on it. That will ALWAYS get you in the "do not use" pool of applicants.

5. Guys and gals, pajama tops or bottoms are not acceptable. I'm not sure when the culture changed and it became acceptable to wear pajamas in public, but it is not appropriate in the world of applying, interviewing or working.

6. Guys and gals, do NOT just wear boxer shorts to apply and interview in. I have heard on more than one occasion of women in the staffing/temporary agency world sharing stories of interviewing a guy and noticing their "stuff" through the opening in the boxer shorts. WEAR PANTS!!!!!!!

7. Guys and gals, if you must wear jeans instead of a nice pair of dress pants please make sure they aren't ripped up or have holes in them.

Please keep in mind that my goal in sharing these items with you is not to be legalistic but to provide you some guidance on how to have the best opportunity to be selected for a job or assignment. Keep in mind that as a staffing/temporary agency, our goal is to select the best applicant, every time, for every job order that a client gives us because we want to keep a good relationship with our clients. If you come in to apply and interview and are not in compliance with the seven points listed above then your chances for a position decrease dramatically. I don't expect you to wear a suit and tie guys, or a beautiful dress ladies…but let's at least be practical okay…enough said.

Application/reflection questions:

1. Have you ever gone into a situation where you later found out that what you were wearing was not appropriate? (Or have you seen this happen to other people?)

2. What were the consequences of you or someone else wearing inappropriate clothing at work, an event or anywhere else?

3. Consider your present situations (work, personal etc.) and evaluate if what you wear is considered appropriate.

CHAPTER 8
The Texting Song (Slumber Party Girls - 2006)

The year of writing for this book, if you haven't figured it out so far, is 2009. I can't recall exactly what year text messaging became the rave but I know that I resisted texting for a long time. I don't want to go into all the reasons why I resisted it but I did resist it for quite a long time. In fact, I know that for several years now I have resisted it. But, about four months or so prior to the start date of writing this book I succumbed to the text messaging age. And, since I have begun text messaging I have found it to be a good way of communication…although sometimes I do get frustrated with all the abbreviations that I have yet to learn. There are a lot of practical ways, both personally and professionally, that texting has streamlined communications for me. In addition to the streamlined communications in texting, it does seem like a large percentage of people now have cell phones. I do realize that not all people have cell phones and/or do not utilize text messaging. If you are a non texting cell phone user, please don't tune me out…this chapter still applies to you.

The whole point of this short chapter is that I want to encourage ALL of you (texters or non texters) to leave your cell phones in the car when you come in to apply or interview. I can't tell you how annoying it is for Human Resource professionals when in the middle of an interview an applicant's cell phone starts ringing. And, even more annoying… disappointing, and aggravating…is to have that applicant ANSWER their cell phone while they are being interviewed. What message do you think you, as an applicant, are sending to the Human Resource professional that is interviewing you? That's right…that talking to your BFF on the phone is more important than getting a job. Also, not appropriate during an interview is reading text messages or sending text messages…as I've said, just leave your cell phone in the car while applying and/ or interviewing.

While I am on the topic of cell phones I want to make a couple more points for you to consider.

Cell Phone Additional Point #1- If for some reason you choose to go against my "leaving your cell phone in the car" recommendation, at least turn it off or put it on vibrate or silent while you are in the office applying and/or interviewing. It is very frustrating and aggravating when a Human Resources professional is interviewing someone and in the middle of the interview, from the front lobby, someone's cell phone starts ringing to the tune of "Sweet Home Alabama" which has the effect of interrupting the flow of the interview in the back of the office. Now, don't get me wrong, I love "Sweet Home Alabama" by Lynrd Skynrd and I'm not trying to offend my fellow Alabamians but really, any song is inappropriate to go off on your cell phone while in the temporary/staffing agency office. And, by the way, I've heard a lot of REALLY, REALLY inappropriate (language/lyrics) songs go off on cell phones in the staffing/temporary agency office. Also, if you are not familiar with staffing/temporary agencies, some staffing/temporary agency offices do not have private offices to interview applicants in so the point of the cell phones blaring music is very appropriate.

Cell Phone Additional Point #2- When you apply with a staffing/ temporary agency (or any business) one of the personal items we ask for when you apply is all of your contact numbers (including your cell phone). We do this so we are able to make contact with you as soon as possible when we have a job order/assignment that is a match for you. When you give out your cell phone number to us…. please make sure of a couple things: 1) Do NOT play tricks with your voice mail message!!!!! What do I mean by "playing tricks?" Well, like recording on your voice mail message, "Hello (long pause) Hello (long pause) Hello (long pause)…Hahahaha guess you just figured out I'm not answering…" That type of message really makes Human Resource professionals upset because our time is very valuable and you are wasting it by making us wait to leave you a message. There have been times when I have not left an applicant a message about a job and went to the next person on the list because of a voice mail message. 2) Do NOT put songs with nasty, offensive lyrics and/or words as your cell phone "wait" tone…I don't want to hear it and I also might pass you up on a job because of it. It is offensive to some people, myself included, to hear all those nasty, offensive lyrics and words.

Cell Phone Additional Point #3- When you change your phone numbers (whether cell phone, home phone or message phone) notify the staffing/temporary agency as soon as possible. It is very frustrating when we try to contact you about a job assignment and cannot reach you.

CHAPTER 9
Crazy Train (Ozzy Osbourne – 1980)

Staffing/temporary agencies can vary widely in the applicant/ candidate flow of each branch office. And, even if a staffing/ temporary agency has a low flow of applicant traffic overall, it never seems to fail that all the activity in one day is confined to the space of about one hour out of the eight hour day (craziness). Recently, we had an applicant come into the staffing agency branch office to apply for work when the lobby was full. The staffing specialist at the front desk greeted the applicant and went through the normal routine of conversation and instruction about how the process worked. One of the policies to proceed through the application process is to provide two forms of identification that satisfy the U.S. Immigrations and Customs Enforcement (ICE) or USCIS I-9 form requirements that prove the applicant meets eligibility requirements to work in the United States. We even have a display copy of the I-9 form which lists the acceptable documents at the front desk so applicants can review it. On this day the applicant I am speaking of did not have both of those documents with him. He proceeded to give the staffing specialist at the front desk grief because he was not allowed to continue with the application process until he produced the required documents. He just kept repeating over and over to the staffing specialist "That's crazy, that's crazy, that's crazy." The staffing specialist confirmed over and over again that the documents had to be provided. Finally, the applicant left the office. The staffing specialist, per the company's policy, documented the conversation in our internal software system for all of us in the office to view if the applicant returned or called in.

Well, sure enough, the "That's crazy" applicant returned later in the day. When this applicant returned and produced the correct forms of identification I, as the area manager for this office, was made aware of the interaction earlier in the day, as well as the notes in our software system and the fact that he had returned. I asked the applicant to come to my desk and I quizzed him about the conversation/interaction he had with the front desk staffing specialist. He recounted the previous conversation to me in a mild, subdued and generally nice way. I then shared with him what the notes in our system indicated and he played it off that he was just frustrated and wasn't lashing out at the staffing specialist. However, the staffing specialist had a different opinion of it. The staffing specialist's opinion was that he was being rude and argumentative with her. I explained to the applicant that based on the staffing specialist's assessment of the "situation" earlier in the day that she felt he was being rude and argumentative. Once again he played it off otherwise. I further explained to the "That's crazy" applicant that based on my staff member's assessment of the situation I would not be willing to place him on an assignment (give him a job)…to which he left quietly.

Alright…now that you have the scenario that I documented in the previous two paragraphs in mind, why do you think that I was so quick to dismiss this applicant and not give him a chance to be placed on an assignment? (Seriously…please take some time to think about this question before you read my answers below).

Reason #1- First of all, my staff members are all professionals, each one is well trained and has successfully studied for and passed the examination to hold the credential of CSP or Certified Staffing Professional. Each staff member is a trusted, valued and appreciated member of my team and they understand the tendencies, attitudes, demeanor and spirit of applicants/candidates. Bottom line…I trust my staff members opinions and evaluations of applicants/candidates.

Reason #2- I did not appreciate how the "That's crazy" applicant treated a trusted, valued & appreciated member of my team. It would undermine the relationship I have built with my staff member if I just said "Oh well" and dismissed the applicant's tirade.

Reason #3- Based on the scenario I laid out in the introduction of this chapter, I explained that the "That's crazy" applicant treated the front desk staffing specialist in a rude and argumentative way but treated me well. What do you find wrong with this picture? I find a lot wrong with it. Sometimes, people (applicants and candidates included) feel like they can treat people who are in what may be regarded as subordinate or lower positions in one way while they treat people that are regarded in a superior or higher position in a different way. This is completely offensive to me.

Reason #4- Based on my reasoning so far, why would I want to reward a "That's crazy" type of applicant by placing them in a job assignment when there are other more qualified, respectful applicants available.

Reason #5- As I have mentioned earlier in this book, I have an obligation to my company and my clients to perform my job well, with diligence and excellence. Placing a candidate such as "That's crazy" would not benefit my company or my client's company. In fact, it would be detrimental to both organizations. How, you ask? First, based on the rude, argumentative behavior of "That's crazy," his tendencies to be rude and argumentative would more than likely rear their ugly head at a client during a difficult or stressful time while on assignment. The consequence of that to my company is that I have an unhappy client who is going to call me and request that "That's crazy" not return on assignment. Second, it will be detrimental to my organization because all the time and money we invested in "That's crazy" will be lost as a result of having to end his assignment. Then, one of two things happen…1) the client will ask for a replacement (hopefully they would ask for a replacement) and then my company has to invest more time and money selecting someone else and getting them ready or 2) the client will be so frustrated with the service and quality it has received from my organization that they may decide not to utilize our services any longer…this is the worst possible outcome of the two case scenarios.

So now that I have presented this situation to you I want to give you some more information that will tie it all together for you. So, let's go back to the initial conversation/interaction between "That's crazy" and the front desk staffing specialist. "That's crazy" treated the front desk staffing specialist with disrespect by being rude and argumentative. Putting this in farming terms, let's call what he did "sowing" which is terminology for planting. Then, "That's crazy" was confronted with his actions by me and I informed him that we would not be placing him on assignment anywhere. Putting this in farming terms, let's call that "reaping" which is farming terminology for harvesting or yielding something. In Galatians 6:7-10 it says:

> "Do not be deceived: God cannot be mocked. A man reaps what he sows. The one who sows to please his sinful nature, from that nature will reap destruction; the one who sows to please the Spirit, from the Spirit will reap eternal life. Let us not become weary in doing good, for at the proper time we will reap a harvest if we do not give up. Therefore, as we have opportunity, let us do good to all people, especially to those who belong to the family of believers."

The point to this chapter, as backed up by Scripture, is that you will reap (get out of it, harvest, yield) what you sow (put into it, plant). The bottom line is that "That's crazy" did not treat the staffing specialist well and it resulted in him not even being considered for a job assignment. I can't tell you how many times I have seen a front desk staffing specialist treated rudely and it end up in the applicant not even being considered. I urge you, to treat all people "good" (as Gal. 6:10 says) and you will reap positive benefits. Don't treat anyone as though they are a lesser person (this just proves that you are on the crazy train). This principle applies everywhere in life, not just in order to get a job. We should treat people well every day.

Application/reflection questions:

1. After reflecting on the actions, words, attitudes and behavior of the "That's crazy" applicant, do you find yourself at times treating some people the same way as "That's crazy" did (being rude and argumentative)?

2. If you now realize that you have been treating some people rudely and with an argumentative nature, what steps do you need to take to make things right with that person or persons?

3. What steps do you need to take to protect yourself from future incidents of treating people rudely and using an argumentative tone?

4. After reading the "Reason" section in this chapter, do you identify yourself at times as classifying, categorizing or viewing certain people, types of people or people with a certain occupation as being lower or less valued than others?

5. If you find yourself categorizing people in this way, what steps do you need to take to end this practice in your life?

CHAPTER 10
U Can't Touch This (MC Hammer – 1990)

Riding in the back seat of the vehicles I referenced in Chapter 1 as a child and young person there were many different "games" we would play while taking a trip somewhere. It didn't really matter if the trips were short ones or long ones…we just enjoyed passing the time playing games. Sometimes these games were brought with us from our house but sometimes they were typical travel games that you may also have played such as the ABC game where you progress through the alphabet from A to Z by finding road signs that have some word that starts with each letter of the alphabet (you have to go in order from A to Z). This is a game that Vickie and I have passed on to our oldest son Jake and we play it sometimes as we take road trips…although Vickie doesn't like me participating while I'm driving as it can cause the driver to become distracted. Although, it's probably safer than talking on the cell phone or texting while driving…I hear that SOME people do that.

However, the travel game that I really enjoyed playing from the back seat as a child and young person was the SLUG BUG game. For those of you not familiar with the SLUG BUG game I'll explain it for you. Every time you saw a Volkswagen Beetle (or BUG) you could rear back and slug the other person in the arm. Thus, the name of the game is SLUG BUG. It didn't matter who was in the backseat with me I would gladly participate. (I didn't even discriminate against playing with my sister.) But, one of the rules in the SLUG BUG game is that there are no SLUG BACKS. What does that mean, no SLUG BACKS? Well, quite simply it means that only one slug could be delivered for every one Volkswagen Beetle (or BUG) spotted. The person who was the recipient of the SLUG could not retaliate by calling "SLUG BUG" on the same Volkswagen BUG. Okay...so this is a fun story you say...but where are you going with this Alan? Hang with me and I'll show you.

Most businesses and organizations these days have employee guidebooks or associate handbooks. Included in these guidebooks or handbooks are all the policies and procedures that you as an employee or associate are responsible for abiding by. One of the policies in the guidebook or handbook will vary in name or title but is usually referred to as physical violence or contact, mutual respect or retaliation. The point is that most organizations have included in this section of their handbook a comment about having zero tolerance for physical violence and possibly even threats of physical violence. The SLUG BUG story ties into this policy.

As you probably have already gathered, I have been involved with, either personally or through my staff members, in the investigations of more physical violence or threat "situations" than I would like to think about. The bottom line is that in most of these instances, the employees or associates that instigated the physical violence or made threats were terminated immediately upon discovering the positive evidence in the investigation process. *You should NEVER lay your hands on another employee or associate in the workplace.*

But, the story goes even deeper, in many of these "situations" the employee or associate that was the one hit, retaliates in some way by either hitting, pushing or shoving the employee or associate that instigated the situation. The sad truth is that the employee or associate that retaliated, or physically defended himself, in many cases was also terminated (remember there are no "slug backs"). This may sound harsh or unfair but there is ABSOLUTELY NO place for laying your hands on another employee or associate in the workplace. Even if you feel that you were unjustly the recipient of physical violence or threats of physical violence, you only have one responsibility in that situation. That one responsibility is to back away (or as I like to say…not engage with the other associate) and inform your supervisor or human resources department as soon as possible.

But, there is one other topic with regard to "U Can't Touch This" that I want to talk about.

In most businesses that I have been involved with (either directly working as an employee for them or serving them as a client of the business I was employed by) there was or is currently another type of "physical" touching going on. Let me give you another FACT not FICTION "situation" to illustrate my point.

It happens every day, singles finding their match on a "dating" website (sounds like a commercial right?). But, in the workplace, singles and married people alike (Oh yes, it happens) find someone that they are, shall we say, "interested" in at the workplace. Many times this "interest" in another person starts off with some sort of talking between the two people, but eventually it leads to flirtatious comments, actions, behavior or contact. In these beginning stages of workplace "interest" (before it becomes a "situation") usually both parties are agreeable to the interactions that are occurring. However, sometime down the road, one or the other of the parties involved gets to the point where they don't want to continue with the "interaction." This is where my staff and I have to step in to deal with the "situation." At this point, one party wants out of the interaction but the other doesn't and there is still physical contact going on. The interaction continues and escalates to a point where the party that wants out decides the only way they can get out is by taking the issue to their supervisor or the Human Resources professionals in their organization. At this point it is now a "situation" to be investigated (Oh...I'm going to throw in another song for you to reference for this point, "Good Lovin' Gone Bad" by Bad Company - 1974). And, depending on the outcome of the investigation, there is usually some sort of disciplinary action taken against the offending associate. This disciplinary action can go from a coaching or counseling all the way up to the termination of employment depending on the specifics of the "situation." By the way this type of "situation" usually falls under the "Harassment" policy of your employer. The point to this message is once again... *You should NEVER lay your hands on another employee or associate in the workplace.* I caution you to be careful even as it relates to friendly hugs or touching fellow associates or employees. I have seen situations where long term friends who were okay with this type of touching occurring inside and outside the workplace in the past suddenly, for one reason or another, decided it is no longer okay. Once again, this is how "situations" that we have to investigate begin.

I have included below a list of some of the "situations" that either I have had to deal with directly or one of my staff members had to deal with. You would do well to steer away from this type of activity in the workplace.

1. At one client, due to the nature of the product manufactured and the machinery used to manufacture the product there were a lot of "pinch points" in the manufacturing processes and products where an associate could get pinched and injured. The client used stickers that said "Warning: Pinch Point" to indicate the hazards in the production processes and products. One of our temporary associates took the "pinch point" stickers and placed them strategically on selected areas of their body (I'll let you decide which areas of HER body you think she put them).

2. I have had staff members have to deal with allegations (which were later proven true) of temporary associates exposing certain body parts to other associates (once again, I'll let you decide which areas of HIS body you think he exposed).

3. I have had "situations" where ex-boyfriends and ex-girlfriends brought allegations that the other party was harassing them either physically or verbally in the workplace.

4.   I have had "situations" where associates reported instances of other associates putting hands in their pockets or in other areas of their clothing.

5.   I have had complaints from associates regarding other associates in the workplace who were having physical contact in break areas, bathrooms or other strategic locations in the facility.

6.   Once, in an orientation, I was talking about the "mutual respect" policy as it related to physical contact. I shared some of the things that are in this chapter. I starting talking about what their responsibility would be if someone else in the workplace hit, pushed, shoved or had any other physical contact with them. Of course, the correct answer to what your responsibility would be is to back away or not engage with the other associate and inform your supervisor or human resources department as soon as possible (you know this because I already shared it earlier in the chapter). However, one of the prospective new hires that was hoping to get a job by attending the orientation immediately belted out "I'd hit them back." After getting over my initial shock that the prospect had said that, I redirected the orientation participants back to the correct answer. And, needless to say (and most importantly) the person that said "I'd hit them back" was never placed on an assignment because of their aggressive nature.

I could go on and on with examples of "situations" but I think you get the picture by now...there are ALWAYS consequences to these types of actions. So, I close this chapter once again by saying…*You should NEVER lay your hands on another employee or associate in the workplace.* By "laying your hands on," I mean in a violent, sensual, flirtatious, teasing, joking, horseplay or any other manner. If you refrain from touching people in the workplace you will never have to deal with the negative consequences that follow these behaviors or actions.

Application/reflection questions:

1. What "situations," as it pertains to physical violence or other physical contact, have you seen in the workplace that turned out to be problems for the associates involved?

2. What lessons have you learned from observing those "situations" and the resulting consequences of those "situations"?

3. Like the guy in the orientation that said "I'd hit them back," do you have physically aggressive tendencies that you need to get under control?

4. After reading this chapter and seeing the possible negative consequences of physical contact in the workplace (including friendly hugging, patting etc.) what steps do you need to take to protect yourself and make sure that you don't become involved in Human Resources having to investigate something that you are doing?

CHAPTER 11
Once Bitten, Twice Shy (Great White - 1989)

In chapter 4 I provided some information that showed the importance of leaving your employer well, specifically as it pertains to future employers and getting good reference checks. But, in this chapter, I want to dive a little further into this topic and show you some other information and perspectives. As a temporary/staffing agency, we have relationships with many different businesses in our local areas. This will either be a benefit to applicants (as we can consider you for placement/assignment at multiple businesses) or it will be a disadvantage to you. How, you say, can it be a disadvantage for you? Well, let me share a story with you that will illustrate how this can be a disadvantage for you. In FACT (not FICTION), the story I share with you in the rest of this chapter is something that happened the very day I began writing this chapter.

I received a phone call from an associate that we had placed at a very large employer in our market. The associate, who we will call "Quitting Quincy" to protect his identity, told me that he was quitting his assignment (without notice) at this very large client. Quitting Quincy had left work early the previous Wednesday stating he was sick and then partially followed absence call in procedures for notification on Thursday and Friday. However, he did not follow absence call in procedures at all on Saturday (a mandatory workday) or the following Monday. Quitting Quincy told me that he had decided, for personal reasons that I will not go into, that he could not in the future (the future mind you) work the assigned shift rotation schedule at the client where he was on assignment at. I quizzed Quitting Quincy regarding the call in procedures and why he did not follow them and he did not have a response. So, in summary, Quitting Quincy did not follow written call in procedures fully on two days and partially on two other days and did not provide the required notice of his intention to quit based on our company's policy. This notification of intention to quit policy is in effect so our staffing company can adequately serve our client by supplying a replacement associate in a timely manner.

However, Quitting Quincy had a further motive for leaving this client without notice. Quitting Quincy promptly stated to me that he knew about another of my clients that had a different shift schedule that would be accommodating to his personal schedule. Furthermore, Quitting Quincy stated that at this other client one of his VERY close relatives held a VERY high ranking position and this relative instructed Quitting Quincy to call me to be placed at this client. What do you think is wrong with this scenario?

Alan's answer to what is wrong with this scenario is…If I have you placed on assignment at a client and you stop coming to work, don't follow call in procedure and then quit without notice, don't expect me to place you at another client even though you try to play a trump card that your VERY close relative holds a VERY high ranking position at the other client. Homey don't play that game!!!!! (Homey D. Clown/Damon Wayans…In Living Color) Why would I want to reward your negative behavior with a positive action? The answer is…I won't. You will only be positively rewarded for positive behavior. As the song title of this chapter says…"Once Bitten, Twice Shy." For those of you not familiar with this saying, I quote from Wikipedia "Once bitten, twice shy is a proverb advising that trust, once betrayed, is not easily restored." If you don't prove yourself as a faithful, diligent associate/employee/worker the first time, I'm certainly not going to trust you with a second chance.

Bottom line…I want to leave you with something you will remember about always leaving an employer or an assignment at a staffing/temporary agency well (on good terms). If you don't leave your assignment well (by not following policies/procedures) and later it comes back to haunt you at the same staffing/temporary agency (or any other business) you will probably beg for "One More Last Chance" (Vince Gill – 1993) but all you will hear from the staffing/temporary agency is "Here's a Quarter - Call Someone Who Cares" (Travis Tritt – 1991).

Application/reflection questions:

1. Have you ever used (or tried to use) manipulation like "Quitting Quincy" to get something you wanted?

2. What were the consequences of your use of manipulation?

3. After considering the material in this chapter, what changes do you need to make in order to not be a manipulative person?

4. Much like "Quitting Quincy" not following policies/procedures, what situations can you recall where you did not follow policies and procedures? What were the consequences of not following those policies and procedures?

CHAPTER 12

[…your love is like] Bad Medicine

(Bon Jovi - 1988)

Once again, I need to share with you a Fact not Fiction situation that occurred at a client location. This situation occurred during the week that I began writing this chapter and is at a location where the company I work for has an onsite supervisory presence in order to handle the volume of activity that is associated with the large number of associates working on assignment there.

The situation began on a Monday afternoon when a man called our office at the client location and one of my staff members (an onsite supervisor) answered the phone. The man identified himself as the "old man" of one of our associates working onsite. The "old man" indicated he was calling in absent for his girlfriend and gave a list of reasons why she would not be at work that day. (Note…the onsite supervisor had a healthy dose of skepticism upon receiving this call and red flags were raised by her…she even sent me an email keeping me informed of this possible "situation.") The associate that the "old man" called about was working second shift during this particular week and did, in fact, report to work on time. However, when she reported to work she was sporting some additional items on her face that had not been there the week before. Those additional items on her face were in the form of stitches that were required subsequent to the physical beating she received over the weekend from the "old man." The associate informed us that she had since left the "old man" and did not want any further contact with him. Furthermore, she stated that her intention was to file a restraining order against him.

During the course of that Monday evening, the "old man" proceeded to contact another of my onsite supervisors and attempt to get a message through to the associate that she needed to come home immediately due to a medical emergency. The onsite supervisor notified the associate and received feedback again that she did not want any contact from the "old man." Over the course of that evening, the "old man" left over 20 messages on our voice mail indicating in various ways and with some very colorful language that he would continue to call until the message got through to the associate. At this point, our client's security team was called in to listen to the messages. I was made aware of all this information by email and was fully prepared the next day for anything that might happen.

As you would imagine, the "old man" called me the next morning (although he did not identify himself as the "old man," I knew who he was by recognizing his voice after having listened to his over 20 voice mail messages from the evening before). In the very first sentence he uttered to me, out of his mouth flew a word that Ralphie from the 1983 movie Christmas Story best describes as the following…

"Only I didn't say 'Fudge.' I said THE word, the big one, the queen-mother of dirty words, the 'F-dash-dash-dash' word!"

When the "old man" dropped this word on me (I refer to it as the F bomb), I immediately stopped him and explained that I did not tolerate profanity and the next time I heard profanity I would promptly hang up the phone. Well, it didn't stop the "old man" and in the next 10 seconds he dropped another profane word on me that describes the excrement of a male bovine and is abbreviated with the letters B & S. Upon hearing this second curse word I immediately hung up the phone. Within a matter of seconds, he called me back and apologized for his profanity. I then inquired if he was the same person that had left over 20 messages the night before that was littered with profanity. He confessed that he was. I explained that, based on the associate's request, we would not be delivering any of his messages to her and that it was in his best interest to not call back again as we would not deal with him. Needless to say, it didn't stop him and I had the privilege of speaking with him two more times that day. Additionally, that night, the "old man" left 24 voice mail messages from shortly after 9:00 pm until almost 2:00 am.

Needless to say, this story has, as its basis, the essence of the title of the 1974 Bad Company Song "Good Lovin' Gone Bad." I don't know the history of this couple's relationship but at some point it went downhill. And, when it went downhill, it had severe consequences for both the associate and the "old man." In addition to not knowing the history of this couple's relationship, I also don't know the Fact or Fiction status of some of the allegations that both the associate and the "old man" made to me, my onsite supervisors or my client's security team. Some of the allegations involved arrests, illegal drug use and legal prescription medication issues. In these situations, it is many times difficult to discern where the truth ends and the lies begin. At the end of the week my staff and I had spoken directly with the "old man" over a dozen times, received over 90 voice mail messages from him which literally took hours to listen to, had to meet with the associate numerous times to ensure she was taking the appropriate steps to protect herself (as well as have us help her to be protected at the worksite), had contact with local police departments and blocked telephone numbers. Additionally, the next week I had to spend more time dealing with this "situation" by filing a restraining order against the "old man."

Here are some of the takeaways for you to treasure after reading my description of this "situation."

1. If you have a "Bad Case of Loving You" (Robert Palmer - 1979) situation, don't let it spill over into the workplace. The worksite is (I know you will find this to be a revelation) for work…not soap opera type antics. The time, energy, resources and frustration spent by me, my staff, my client's management and my client's security staff were not productive uses of time. When we have to focus on non central issues like this, it takes the emphasis off of those revenue driving activities such as making a product or providing a service. This is never healthy for an organization.

2. False accusations, statements or outright lies will not get you anywhere. It is always best to tell the truth. Although, in this situation, I was never able to come to a complete resolution as to who was telling the truth, and it did not

cost anyone their job, there have been many situations where I or my staff have proven associates to be liars and it cost them their job. If you will remember the following statement it will benefit you greatly as it pertains to the workplace…. "Liar, Liar = Fire, Fire." There is no upside to lying. When you are found out to be a liar, there will be dire consequences…you will get fired. As an example, once we had two associates that lied about their whereabouts during work hours. No one from the client could find these two associates even though they knew where the two associates were supposed to be. It was ultimately proven that these two associates were somewhere besides where they were supposed to be (and where they stated during the investigation that they were). In the end, these associates lost their jobs.

3. Profanity has no place at the worksite. I know that the example I gave was of the "old man" who was not an associate of the company I work for, but I can assure you that the same profane words (and other inappropriate language) have been used by associates and it resulted in disciplinary action. Most employers view this type of language as a violation of the mutual respect policy as it pertains to "creating an intimidating, hostile or offensive work environment." It is never beneficial for you to use this type of language on the job.

Application/reflection questions:

1. Would you say that you are a person who uses profanity (foul language, cussing etc), never, seldom, occasionally or frequently?

2. If you answered question one with anything other than "never," do you realize based on reading this chapter the importance of refraining from this type of language in the workplace? If so, what steps do you need to take to end the practice of using profanity in the workplace?

3. Would you say that you are a person who, in the workplace, tells lies 1) never 2) seldom 3) occasionally or 4) frequently?

4. If you answered question three with anything other than "never," do you realize based on reading this chapter the importance of refraining from lying in the workplace? If so, what steps to you need to take to end the practice of lying in the workplace?

5. What steps, if any, do you need to take in order to prevent any or all of your relationships from going bad and spilling over into the workplace?

Proverbs 12:22 (New Living Translation)

"The LORD detests lying lips, but he delights in those who tell the truth."

Ephesians 5:4 (English Standard Version)

"Let there be no filthiness nor foolish talk nor crude joking, which are out of place, but instead let there be thanksgiving."

ALAN BALMER

CHAPTER 13

Call Me (Blondie - 1980) and Don't Call Us, We'll Call You (Sugarloaf – 1975)

Since the word "call" appears in the chapter title 3 times, you may have guessed that this chapter will be all about the telephone (ding ding ding…you're a winner). In this chapter, I will give you several different aspects regarding the telephone. You might be thinking that the two song titles that identify this chapter are contradictory. However, I will give you information that ties in both song titles… specifically about when to call and when to NOT to call.

Most companies have a policy that outlines the associate's role as it pertains to being absent and calling in to notify the company of that absence. The absence policy usually reads something like this…"All associates are required to notify the company by calling in each and every day they will be absent, late or leave early." In addition, the policy usually goes further by giving the associate information such as the number to call in to, who to ask for and the criteria for making sure that the call in is done in a timely manner.

Why is it so important for associates to follow this policy you ask? Let me give you a FACT not FICTION situation that will illustrate. Throughout this book I have referenced a client where the company I work for has had a very large number of temporary associates on assignment. This client literally has a total of multiple thousands of full time associates, as well as temporary associates working at their facility. The client is in the manufacturing business (not a service based business) so their core objective is to maximize the available working hours to manufacture the product that they will place in the market for consumers to purchase. It is with regard to this "maximizing the available working hours" that I want to give you some insight into.

Daily, almost without exception, at this client either my company or my client company will have associates that fail to call in reporting either that they will be absent for the day or be late. The first consequence of the associate's failure to follow this policy is that my client runs the risk of not being able to start the production line at the designated start time of each shift. If my client is not able to start the production line at the designated start time of each shift, there could literally be thousands of associates not engaged in the production process because the line could not start up. These thousands of associates will just be standing around (while being paid) waiting for the line to start. So, let's think about the consequences (for both my client company and the associates) that occur as a result of the line not starting at the designated time.

Consequence #1- For the business, they will not be able to manufacture any product that can be sent to the market during this down time. Summary…less product to the market, less revenue for the business.

Consequence #2- For the business, they still have the obligation to pay the thousands of associates that are standing around for the precious minutes that no product is being manufactured. Summary…less product to the market, less revenue for the business, but still having to pay the expenses for labor (associates).

Consequence #3- For the associates, the first 2 consequences affect the overall profitability of the company which in turn has the effect of limiting the available resources (money) that is available to be used in the future to pay for associate's pay raises, health insurance, dental insurance, life insurance, retirement plans etc. You see, the company is in business to make a profit. And, if the company is not profitable or possibly even profitable but not meeting the expectations of the owners or shareholders, this will have a negative affect on the associate's future compensation and benefit allocation amounts.

Therefore, I want to make sure you understand just how important it is for you to call in when you are absent. When you know you are going to be out, please, please, please follow your employer's guidelines and policies for calling in. At the moment you realize you are going to be late to work, please, please, please call in to notify the business of how late you will be. It is in the overall best interest of you and your employer to maximize the output during the available working hours. This applies for both manufacturing and service based businesses. As the song by Blondie says "Call Me" when you know you are going to be out of work for the entire day or even a part of the day.

So now you understand the importance of calling in to report your absences and late occurrences but there is another aspect of the telephone that I want to talk about. In order to get this point across, let me give you another FACT not FICTION situation regarding this large client I have been referring to. Part of the process for getting associates ready for this client is to have a large orientation where information is given out to prepare the associates and ensure they are ready to go on the assignment at this client. At points in history we have had over one hundred people fully through this orientation process and ready to start on assignment. However, one roadblock still exists for them to start on assignment at this large client. That roadblock is that we have to receive an order from the client asking for the associates to start work on a specific date. Sometimes we are able to start the associates the next day after the orientation and sometimes it is literally a matter of weeks or months before we can get them started. When my staff and I conduct these orientations, we communicate very clearly to the candidates that are in the orientation that as soon as we have an order from the client we will contact them because we need them to start work as badly as they want to start work. See, we are evaluated by the client regularly on many different areas but one of those is on fill rate. The fill rate is the percentage of orders we fill in the requested timeframe. We always want a 100 percent fill rate.

As I mentioned, we inform the candidates in orientation that we will call them as soon as we have an order. However, we are well aware of the fact that many times these candidates are very antsy, anxious and anticipatory of starting as soon as they can in order to have income. Since we have this awareness, we do inform the candidates that if they would like to call me once per week to check in they can do so. In this portion of our communication to the candidates we specifically ask them NOT to call us everyday as it causes difficulty. In spite of these instructions, I can't begin to count the number of times candidates will blow up my phone, calling to check in every day, numerous times per day. This is very, very, very frustrating to me.

So, let's think about the consequences (for both me and you) that occur as a result of calling me every day, numerous times per day, in spite of my explicit instructions to not do so.

Consequence #1- For me, having more than 100 people in a pool ready to start work, I simply cannot handle the daily calls of 100 or more people. I would literally get nothing else done in the day except answering phone calls and talking to candidates. This causes me frustration, aggravation and has the effect of making me very inefficient in my job duties.

Consequence #2- For you, calling in every day, multiple times per day in spite of the instructions I have given out to call in only once per week signals to me that you are unable to follow instructions. And, if you are unable to follow my instructions, most likely you won't be able to follow the instructions, policies or guidelines of my company or my client company. If you are unable to follow instructions, policies or guidelines, why would I place you on assignment when I know that it will cause "situations" down the road that I will have to deal with? The answer is that I won't place you on assignment if you can't follow instructions.

So, when I (or anyone else for that matter) give you a set of instructions about when and how frequently to call in, please follow them. If I tell you I will call you, follow the premise of the song title and realize the Sugarloaf song title "Don't Call Us, We'll Call You" is appropriate.

Oh...and one more important piece of telephone etiquette information. If somehow, as an associate or applicant, you obtain my cell phone number, don't call me during non business hours and especially weekends.

Application/reflection questions:

1. Would you say that you are a person who has in the past either not called in to report your absences or late occurrences per your company's policies?

2. If you answered question one yes, do you now understand the importance of following this company policy?

3. Similar to my story of candidates calling in every day when instructed not to, for you what work "situations" can you think of that you personally did not follow (or are not currently following) your employers instructions? What negative consequences have resulted from those "situations" you can recall?

ALAN BALMER

CHAPTER 14
Beggin' (Frankie Valli and the Four Seasons - 1966) The story of a beggar, a bill and a business card

At the first staffing company I worked for as an Area Manager, I had the responsibility for sales and operations in three branch offices that were located within about a one hour driving distance of each other. I would routinely travel the same set of interstates and two lane state roads to get to each branch. Over a period of several weeks when I first began traveling this route, I noticed a man begging for money at the same interstate exit off ramp. For various reasons, which may or may not be correct, in the first couple of weeks of seeing this beggar I did not stop to assist him. At this point you might be judging me for not stopping to assist the beggar. I will not try to persuade you with regard to the correctness or incorrectness of my action (really inaction) but I would like to share with you what happened one day when I felt compelled to stop and assist the beggar after the first two weeks of my inaction.

On the day of my stopping to assist the beggar, I rolled up to the red signal light and proceeded to roll my window down. I handed the beggar a five dollar bill so he could purchase a meal but I also began to give the beggar some information that could prove vital to his future. I explained to the beggar who I was and what my job responsibilities were. In summary, I told the beggar that I worked for a staffing company that was looking to recruit people to work for companies that needed workers. I handed the beggar my business card and asked him to come visit me in that town's staffing agency branch office (located just a few short blocks from the interstate off ramp exit where I had seen him begging for the last two weeks). I further explained that I would like to help him find work so that he would not have to beg.

There are two things that I would like to share with you that happened subsequent to the verbal exchange that I had with the beggar that day. The first thing I want to share is that the beggar never ever came to the staffing agency branch office to see me or anyone of my staff to apply for employment. The second thing I want to share is that, in spite of my almost daily travels utilizing the same interstate exit off ramp, I never ever saw the beggar at that location again (or any other location for that matter).

Now, I don't know the actual reason why the beggar never came to the branch office to apply or never showed back up begging at the interstate exit off ramp. There could be many reasons that we could speculate about with regard to where the beggar went but, I have always felt deep down in my heart that the beggar knew that I had called him out and that he would no longer be able to fly under the radar. Please keep in mind that I am not judging the beggar but I honestly felt like he could have been working rather than begging…there were plenty of jobs available at that time.

There is an important principle that I want to share with you regarding this situation. In chapter 6 I shared with you some passages from the Bible in the book of Proverbs that talked about the importance of working, and doing so with excellence. However, I need to share one more passage of Scripture with you that will have far ranging impact for you.

2 Thessalonians 3:10-12 (NIV)

"For even when we were with you, we gave you this rule: "If a man will not work, he shall not eat." We hear that some among you are idle. They are not busy; they are busybodies. Such people we command and urge in the Lord Jesus Christ to settle down and earn the bread they eat."

First, with regard to this Scripture passage, let me tell you that I DO understand that there are situations where people are not able to work. These situations can include personal medical issues, lack of available work, family issues or transportation issues as well as other reasons. However, based on my experience and understanding of 16 plus years in Human Resources, I know of hundreds and hundreds of situations where people chose not to work for reasons that are not valid. For example, as of the writing of this book, the state in which I reside has an unemployment rate which is over 10%. With an unemployment rate over 10% there ARE people that want to work that can't find a job. I see these applicants on a daily basis these days. However, there are people that won't take work that has been offered to them. I was recently at a seminar for my state's local staffing association and one of the speakers was from the state unemployment office. This speaker shared that when our state's unemployment rate was around the 4% mark about a year ago that this was what the unemployment office referred to as "full employment." He explained that at 4% unemployment, all the people that wanted to work were working. There is something wrong with this scenario.

Anyhow, sometimes people aren't working for reasons that include rate of pay, the type of work not being in their field of training, environment for the work, difficulty of the work or other possibly valid reasons. However, there are also other people that won't take work for other superficial reasons like the type of work, in their opinion, being beneath them, not glamorous enough, in a field of work that is objectionable to them, etc. Can I tell you that the passage of Scripture mentioned previously (2 Thess. 3:10-12) applies to many of these superficial "reasons" I have listed. Let me just tell you that bottom line…if work is available, you are available for work and you have an offer of work, that it is more noble to work and earn your money than to have to beg, live off someone else's hard work or do without because of your "pride." I encourage you to live by this Scripture's principle that YOU SHOULD WORK.

Application/reflection questions:

1. Would you say that you are a person who has either in the past or currently not accepted work because of a "superficial" reason as outlined in this chapter?

2. If you answered question one yes, do you now understand the importance of working for a living rather than begging or sponging off of someone else? If so, what actions do you need to take to seek employment?

3. With regard to beggars and those who are unemployed, what are your personal thoughts and convictions with regard to helping these people out?

Acts 20:35

"In everything I did, I showed you that by this kind of hard work we must help the weak, remembering the words the Lord Jesus himself said: '*It is more blessed to give than to receive.*'"

Proverbs 22:9

"A generous man will himself be blessed, for he shares his food with the poor."

Proverbs 28:27
"He who gives to the poor will lack nothing, but he who closes his eyes to them receives many curses."

ALAN BALMER

CHAPTER 15
Common Sense (John Prine - 1975)

You are about to enter the common sense zone. The common sense zone is all about one of the most memorable associates that I have had the privilege and responsibility of dealing with. The story of this associate follows.

One of my staff members had reported to me that this particular associate had been having difficulty meeting production standards at our client and she had several interactions with the associate which were memorable. In fact, the supervisor at this client had given this associate a below expectations rating on the most recently conducted written evaluation and was still having issues meeting production standards even after additional attempts had been made at providing further training on the processes. I made the decision that I, along with my staff member and the supervisor at the client, would meet with the associate to set a path forward for the resolution of the issue. So, the meeting was scheduled and we brought (well tried to bring) to the attention of the associate the concerns and issues with regard to meeting production standards. For the next 30 minutes, as we tried to explain the issues to the associate, we were bombarded by the associate with a steady dose of head bobbing, eyes rolling, an argumentative nature, rudeness, attitude in the vocal responses given and a lack of attention/focus/listening to the issues we tried to bring. In addition to this bombardment of verbal and nonverbal responses, the associate must have said half a dozen times or more that "good common sense" was an attribute of theirs and that what we were saying to the associate made "no good common sense." The associate, who was henceforth dubbed "Good Common Sense," could not and would not respond to the issues that we presented but just continued to state that they had "Good Common Sense." Ultimately, we had to stop the meeting with the associate with the statement, "Look, if your production does not meet the company standards within two weeks, your assignment will be ended."

Very soon after this meeting, there was a reduction in production announced by this client and all the temporary associates were laid off. During the period between the announcement of the layoff and the actual layoff itself, myself and my staff member had about ten more conversations with "Good Common Sense." These interactions dealt with the topic of a particular benefit that this associate was not eligible for as the criteria for the benefit had not been met. Although we explained the ineligibility and provided documentation of the ineligibility we continued to hear the phrase "no good common sense" over and over and over. In fact, I don't think an interaction with this person went by when we didn't hear this phrase. However, the most disturbing fact was that during these interactions, "Good Common Sense" continued the head bobbing, eyes rolling, attitude giving and lack of listening.

It seemed that no matter what we did there was a lack of respect from this associate. Due to the timing of the impending layoff, we allowed this employee to work until the layoff date.

However, several months down the road, when the production was increased at this client, and we were asked to bring in temporaries to fill the orders, "Good Common Sense" was not offered an invitation to start these brand new assignments at this client even though there were other associates that were laid off that did receive invitations to apply for the new assignments at this client. When this person found out that we were bringing temporaries in for these assignments "Good Common Sense" asked if they could come back. I explained to this person that we would not be extending them an invitation for these assignments. From that day forward I, my staff members and others in my organization had many, many conversations with "Good Common Sense" notifying this person that there would not be an invitation to return due to the following reasons.

1. Argumentative nature of "Good Common Sense" (lack of respect) towards myself, my staff members and my client's staff.

2. Attitude with eyes rolling and head bobbing displayed by this associate.

3. Rudeness in comments and nonverbal signs displayed by "Good Common Sense."

4. In addition to the interpersonal issues listed in #1-3, this associate could not meet production standards at the client.

In addition, after several conversations with "Good Common Sense" explaining why they would not be considered for assignment at this client, I heard the "lawyer" word from this person... remember the chapter on "lawyers" as it pertains to threats? "Good Common Sense" also had conversations with other management members in the organization I worked for and they explained the same thing to this person (that there would not be consideration for assignment at this client). Amazingly enough, even after I and other management members in the organization had multiple conversations with "Good Common Sense" indicating they would not be considered for assignment, I recently received a voice mail message from "Good Common Sense" indicating several things. The first thing in the voice mail message was that this person was notifying me that an application had been made to other companies for employment. The second thing in the voice mail message was "Good Common Sense" asking me that when I received a phone call for a reference request, to give a quote "a pretty decent report" as it related to the past work performance of this associate. Let me tell you that "a pretty decent report" was not and will not be given as it pertains to "Good Common Sense" if and when someone calls me for a reference request.

The moral of this chapter is that you should be respectful, courteous and kind with your employer or, if on a temporary assignment, to the staff of the business where you are placed on assignment. There is absolutely no room for head bobbing, eyes rolling, ignoring, rudeness, argumentation, lack of consideration, lack of attention or any other type of negative interaction when it comes to the workplace. I do understand that people are not always going to agree on a "situation" but there is always something positive that can result if you go into the situation with the right frame of mind.

Keep in mind the following Proverbs from the Bible when it comes to living your life on the straight and narrow, with integrity, consideration and honesty is it pertains to your employer.

Proverbs 10:21 (NLT)

"The words of the godly encourage many, but fools are destroyed by their lack of common sense."

Proverbs 21:16

"The person who strays from common sense will end up in the company of the dead."

Application/reflection questions:

1. Would you say that you are a person who has either in the past or currently (in the workplace or any other place for that matter) displayed an attitude, been rude, been argumentative or not listened to, focused on or considered feedback/criticism that was given to you?

2. If you answered yes to question one, do you now understand the importance of going into every situation with the right frame of mind in order to receive feedback that will help you improve as a worker?

3. Does this story, and the application of it, bring to mind individuals with whom you need to meet with for the purpose of making a situation right and possibly even apologizing?

Philippians 2:14 (NIV)

"Do everything without complaining or arguing."

CHAPTER 16
Hit Me With Your Best Shot
(Pat Benatar – 1979)

The recurring message in each chapter up until now has been how you can and should take personal responsibility to improve your work ethic, work habits and application/ interview skills. I have given you very specific items to work on for your personal improvement plan. But now, in this chapter, I want to move from talking about what your responsibilities are as an applicant, associate or employee to the area of responsibilities that the employer/business has. I know I have touched on this briefly in past chapters but it is worth focusing on again. The Human Resource professionals that are employed by businesses have the responsibility of hiring the BEST applicants/ candidates for every position that is open. By doing so, the Human Resource professional is giving the organization the best chance of maximizing its resources to be a profitable organization (or in the case of a not-for-profit organization of providing the best service level possible). Therefore, based on the principle that businesses want to hire the BEST, if you are not following the suggestions provided thus far in the book, you are decreasing your chances of being viewed as or considered the BEST applicant/candidate for open positions.

In order to paint a picture and etch it in your memory of how important it is to businesses to hire the BEST, I want to walk you through something. But, before I walk you through this, I want to ask you to answer three questions in order to prepare you for the journey through what I want to share with you. So here goes… three questions…please answer them yourself before you move on to the definitions I will provide later.

Question #1 What is a "fool"?

Question #2 When I say the phrase "any passer-by" what do you think of?

Question #3 What is an "archer"?

"Fool" is defined in Merriam-Webster's Collegiate Dictionary-Tenth Edition as several things that are applicable here…

1.   a person lacking in judgment or prudence

2.   a harmlessly deranged person or one lacking in common powers of understanding

In addition, the Harper's Bible Dictionary provides several definitions that you need to consider…

1.   an inability to be cautious in speech

2.   pursuing courses of conduct or action that ultimately prove to be harmful

3.   ...commits specific acts that are detrimental for the person or for society

"Any passer-by" leads me to think of words or phrases like "all-inclusive," "without discretion," "nobody left out" or "each and every person." It makes me think of the times that my wife has shopped at a store in the mall and I sat on a bench waiting for her to get done and just watched people come past me while sitting on the bench. If you have ever just sat and "people watched" you know what "any passer-by" is referring to. It implies to me that anyone and everyone is selected no matter what someone looks like, acts like or talks like. This means including anyone and everyone in whatever it is you are doing...without ever saying "no." By the way, "passer-by" is defined in Merriam Webster's Collegiate Dictionary-Tenth Edition as "one who passes by."

"Archer" is defined in Merriam-Webster's Collegiate Dictionary-Tenth Edition as "a person who uses a bow and arrow."

Okay so I know that for some of you the answers to these three questions have been less than a revelation but for others it will have been very insightful. So, with that little exercise behind us, let me share with you the purpose of this question and answer session... please read the following passage of Scripture.

"Like an archer who wounds at random

is he who hires a fool or any passer-by." (Prov. 26:10)

Let me tell you that this passage of Scripture, as a Human Resource professional, dials in on the essence of why it is so important to hire the "BEST" every single time. First of all, an archer who randomly shoots game to purposefully wound them is not going to be focused, diligent or effective at what they are trying to accomplish. All this random wounding does is to cause pain, grief, discomfort, disability and possibly a slow death in the animals that are being shot. Now, let's take that line of thought about shooting and wounding animals at random and apply it to the second line in Proverbs 26:10. When a Human Resources professional hires fools and passersby without discretion (ie just hiring anybody and everybody without trying to select the BEST) they are doing the same thing to the business that they work for as the archer does to the game that they wound at random. Bottom line is that the Human Resources professional, by hiring fools and passersby, is causing pain, grief, discomfort, disability and possibly a slow death to the business or organization that they are hiring for. The fact of the matter is, that for an archer, they have to be highly focused on the target that they are shooting at in order to accomplish their purpose. The same applies for Human Resource professionals…they must be highly focused on selecting the "BEST" candidate every time in order to accomplish their purpose.

Do you now see why it is so important for Human Resource professionals to be diligent about the performance of their duties? I hope this powerful proverb from the Bible helps to implant in your mind the fact that as a job seeker you must put yourself in a position when applying and interviewing of not appearing to be just another person off the street (any passerby) or fool. You must present yourself to be the "BEST" or your chance of getting a job will be severely handicapped. I hope that the next time you apply or interview that you will give it your best shot.

Application/reflection questions:

1. After reflecting on the issues presented in this book so far, would you honestly consider yourself to be in the "BEST" applicant/candidate category?

2. After reflecting on Proverbs 26:10 in this chapter, would you consider yourself to be a "fool" or "any passerby"?

3. If the answer to question one is no, or the answer to question two is yes, what improvements do you need to make to get into the "BEST" category?

ALAN BALMER

CHAPTER 17
Long Black Train (Josh Turner – 2002) or Stairway to Heaven (Led Zeppelin – 1971)

By now, you have received all the information that I want to communicate in this book as it pertains to "temporary insanity" and not falling into those traps in the future. Therefore, the rest of this chapter is not devoted to those types of instruction. Rather, this chapter is dedicated to making sure that you have a clear understanding of why I have included Bible passages in some of the prior chapters. The Bible has been an instrumental tool that has given me guidance, instruction and purpose for over 20 years. You see, in 1988 I had a profound spiritual experience that has set me on a path forward of trying to be constantly introspective and focus on improving myself. That spiritual experience was being introduced to Jesus Christ. I came to realize through a series of conversations and events that I had to make a change in my life in order to prevent the destruction that was sure to come if I did not. Ultimately, I realized that I had to make a decision about who or what I was going to serve (this is a decision that at some point in every person's life they have to make). It became clear to me that the decision was between the Kingdom of God and the Kingdom of the devil. I realized that the Kingdom of the devil was about spiritual death, bondage and discouragement, while the Kingdom of God was about spiritual life, freedom and encouragement. I made the choice to switch teams from the Kingdom of the devil to the Kingdom of God. In this chapter I want to make sure you have a clear presentation of the Kingdom of God and how you can make certain you are a member of it. In order to help you understand why this "choice" I referred to earlier is so important I want to walk you through a parallel between work situations and spiritual situations.

Why is it so important that you walk through the following paragraphs you might ask? Well, one reason is that many of you reading this book might feel like in your personal lives that you are doing what many do in the workplace...just simply punching the time clock of life each day. Many people in the workplace just punch in and punch out each day with no real sense of purpose... they are just logging time waiting for something to happen. I don't want you to continue to feel like you are just punching the time clock of life everyday. By honestly and sincerely evaluating the following paragraphs in this chapter I know that you can change from just punching the time clock of life to having a passion, zeal and sense of mission, purpose and importance with what you do every day (not just work, but personal as well). I know I can attest from personal experience that if you will put into practice what the rest of this chapter reveals that you will move from a time clock puncher to a life lover.

With regard to walking you through the parallel between work situations and spiritual situations, first I want to talk about you coming to a realization of your PROBLEM. Throughout this book, with regard to "work" issues we have identified and showed many problems that occur for applicants, interviewees and workers. For example, some of the problems that people are afflicted with in the workplace are threatening people, not showing up to work, touching people (or any of the other numerous examples I have given in this book). But, the work arena is not the only place in life where you will deal with problems. In the spiritual realm there are also problems that you have to deal with. In the spiritual, the first problem realization that needs to be achieved is that of sin. With regard to sin, the Bible, in 1 Corinthians 6:9 (NIV) says "Do you not know that the wicked will not inherit the kingdom of God." Furthermore, the Bible gives us a clear understanding of what wickedness is and defines it as sin. In Galatians 5:19-21 we see documented "The acts of the sinful nature are obvious: sexual immorality, impurity and debauchery; idolatry and witchcraft; hatred, discord, jealousy, fits of rage, selfish ambition, dissensions, factions and envy; drunkenness, orgies, and the like. I warn you, as I did before, that those who live like this will not inherit the kingdom of God." According to Galatians 5:21 the spiritual problem of sin automatically puts you in the category of not being able to inherit the Kingdom of God. By the way, Romans 3:23 says "for all have sinned and fall short of the glory of God." In addition, 1 John 1:10 says, "If we claim we have not sinned, we make him out to be a liar and his word has no place in our lives." I want you to understand that the problem of sin is a problem we ALL have to deal with.

Second I want to talk about the results of your PROBLEM. Throughout this book, with regard to "work" issues, we have identified and shown many consequences that are associated with problems that occur. For the examples of workplace problems I listed in the last paragraph the consequences of those problems is that you will more than likely lose your job or be disciplined. I think you understand by now that negative actions will lead to negative consequences as it pertains to work. But, in the spiritual realm, there is a parallel to this workplace cause and effect progression. In the last paragraph, we learned that the spiritual problem of sin automatically puts you in the category of not being able to inherit the Kingdom of God...this is the result of the sin problem. If the "Kingdom of God" is not available to you as a sinner, what is your final destination? Well, Romans 6:23 says "For the wages of sin is death," and, Matthew 5:29-30 documents, "...It is better for you to lose one part of your body than for your whole body to be thrown into hell. And if your right hand causes you to sin, cut it off and throw it away. It is better for you to lose one part of your body than for your whole body to go into hell." Lastly, Revelation 20:12-15 records "And I saw the dead, great and small, standing before the throne, and books were opened. Another book was opened, which is the book of life. The dead were judged according to what they had done as recorded in the books. The sea gave up the dead that were in it, and death and Hades gave up the dead that were in them, and each person was judged according to what he had done. Then death and Hades were thrown into the lake of fire. The lake of fire is the second death. If anyone's name was not found written in the book of life, he was thrown into the lake of fire." I think you can see that the result or consequence of the sin problem is that you are automatically assigned to the Kingdom of the devil where a place in hell is reserved for you. However, there is a way that you can transfer from the Kingdom of the devil to the Kingdom of God.

Third, I want to talk about how you can resolve the problem. With regard to workplace issues the resolution to your problems is that you make a change that puts you back in favor with your employer. Or, as it pertains to applicants and interviewees, you can change your habits, practices, attitudes, way of speech etc. so that your problem of being blocked for job selection is overcome. There are definitely ways to overcome these workplace and application problems. I have shown you those throughout this book and I trust you will put them in place. However, with regard to the spiritual problem of sin and the resulting consequence of being assigned to the Kingdom of the devil, you can overcome this as well. God has provided a way for you to switch teams from the Kingdom of the devil to the Kingdom of God. How you ask? Well, Romans 6:23 says, "For the wages of sin is death, but the gift of God is eternal life in Christ Jesus our Lord." Also, Ephesians 2:8-9 reveals "For it is by grace you have been saved, through faith—and this not from yourselves, it is the gift of God—not by works, so that no one can boast." 1 John 1:9 gives us further instruction that "If we confess our sins, he is faithful and just and will forgive us our sins and purify us from all unrighteousness." Lastly, as far as Scripture is concerned, 2 Corinthians 7:10 tells us regarding confession that "Godly sorrow brings repentance that leads to salvation and leaves no regret, but worldly sorrow brings death." I hope that you can see through the progression of the four Scriptures I have listed in this paragraph that making the decision to move from the Kingdom of the devil to the Kingdom of God is quite simple. By believing in Jesus Christ by faith and confessing your sins to God and asking for forgiveness of those sins you will be led to salvation (the gift of God that moves you from the Kingdom of the devil to the Kingdom of God).

The spiritual problem of sin essentially boils down to the title of this chapter...The Josh Turner song "Long Black Train" talks about being on a train conducted by the devil and how you are automatically on that train because of the problem of sin. That message is much the same as I have communicated in previous paragraphs, that your sin will cause you to go to the destination of hell, or being assigned to the Kingdom of the devil. Although the song "Stairway to Heaven" by Led Zeppelin is by no means a "spiritual" song, Jesus Christ is THE Stairway to Heaven. Only by trusting, relying on and believing in Him will you be able to access the Kingdom of God. You can make the switch from the Kingdom of the devil to the Kingdom of God through Jesus Christ.

Fourth, I want to talk to you about your responsibilities upon resolving your problem and moving from the Kingdom of the devil to the Kingdom of God. With regard to workplace issues you have responsibilities to your employer once you resolve those problems with your employer. Those responsibilities include acting appropriately going forward in order that you might stay in right standing with your employer. Many times this means changing the way you work, act, talk and present yourself...these are the expectations of your employer. However, with regard to the spiritual problem of sin, once you overcome the problem of sin there are responsibilities to God similar to that of correction and adjustment in the workplace. Let me share with you some items from the Bible that will show what your responsibility is upon switching teams from the Kingdom of the devil to the Kingdom of God. Matthew 7:21-23 says "Not everyone who says to me, 'Lord, Lord,' will enter the kingdom of heaven, but only he who does the will of my Father who is in heaven. Many will say to me on that day, 'Lord, Lord, did we not prophesy in your name, and in your name drive out demons and perform many miracles?' Then I will tell them plainly, 'I never knew you. Away from me, you evildoers!'" Next, Romans 14:17-19 records "For the kingdom of God is not a matter of eating and drinking, but of righteousness, peace and joy in the Holy Spirit, because anyone who serves Christ in this way is pleasing to God and approved by men. Let us therefore make every effort to do what leads to peace and to mutual edification." Additionally, 1 John 3:9-10 shows us that "No one who is born of God will continue to sin, because God's seed remains in him; he cannot go on sinning, because he has been born of God. This is how we know who the children of God are and who the children of the devil are: Anyone who does not do what is right is not a child of God; nor is anyone who does not love his brother." Lastly, Matthew 28:18-20 instructs us further in that, "Then Jesus came to them and said, 'All authority in heaven and on earth has been given to me. Therefore go and make disciples of all nations, baptizing them in the name of the Father and of the Son and of the Holy Spirit, and teaching them to obey everything I have commanded you. And surely I am with you always, to the very end of the age.'" I hope you understand from these four Scriptures that action is required upon your decision to change teams from the Kingdom of the devil to the Kingdom of God.

Let me wrap this up by giving you an invitation to move into the Kingdom of God (or as the title of this chapter indicates...to get off the long black train...like the one I was on in early 1988 when I chose the stairway to heaven). Although there is nothing "magic" about the words that follow...if you honestly believe the following items then I'll facilitate the process of introducing you to Jesus Christ just like I was in 1988.

What are your answers to the following questions based on the message of this chapter (especially reflecting on the Bible passages)?

1. Are you a sinner?

2. Do you believe that your sin has caused you to be a passenger on the long black train destined for hell, a participant in the Kingdom of the devil, or as the 1979 ACDC song describes it "The Highway to Hell"?

3. Do you want forgiveness for your sins in order to get off the long black train destined for hell and take the stairway to heaven?

4. Do you believe Jesus died on the cross for you, rose again and that He is the stairway to heaven?

5. Are you willing to surrender your life to Jesus Christ... meaning that you will be obedient to follow his will, stop sinning and work for the Kingdom of God?

6. If you believe and agree with the above, you are ready to pray for the following things.

   a. Pray to invite Jesus into your life and your heart.

   b. Pray to ask Jesus for forgiveness for your sins (to be your Savior).

   c. Pray to ask Jesus for help to stop sinning.

   d. Pray to make a commitment to follow Jesus (to let him by your Lord).

   e. Pray to make a commitment to work for the Kingdom of God instead of the Kingdom of the devil.

I would encourage you at this point if you want to move from the long black train to hell and take the stairway to heaven (Jesus) that you honestly and sincerely from the heart pray through the things that I've listed in point 6 above. In Romans10:9-11 the following is found…

"That if you confess with your mouth, 'Jesus is Lord,' and believe in your heart that God raised him from the dead, you will be saved. For it is with your heart that you believe and are justified, and it is with your mouth that you confess and are saved. As the Scripture says, 'Anyone who trusts in him will never be put to shame.'"

If you prayed, believed and confessed this for the very first time (or are making a recommitment) I congratulate you and welcome you into the Kingdom of God…good choice on taking the "Stairway to Heaven" (Jesus) and getting off the "Long Black Train" or avoiding the "Highway to Hell." I would love to hear from you if you made this choice today…I encourage you to email me at alan.scott.balmer@gmail.com so I can help you in your path forward with God.

ALAN BALMER

CHAPTER 18
The Final Countdown (Europe – 1985)

Well, if you made the decision to pray, believing and confessing Jesus Christ as Lord and Savior, I congratulate you. It was the best decision I ever made and I know it will be for you as well. However, this decision is not the "Final Countdown," rather just the starting point for your new journey for the rest of your life. This decision will impact your life as an employee, applicant and as a person for the rest of your life. Now that you have made this decision, there is a change that has occurred in you and I want to make sure to explain that change as well as the benefits of this change. The reason for pointing out this change is very important in terms of laying a foundation to show you further truths as it pertains to your work ethic, work quality, responsibilities to your employer etc. In order to explain this change, I need you to read the following portion of the Bible found in 2 Corinthians 3:14-18 and then reflect on the points I make afterwards.

2 Corinthians 3:14-18

"But their minds were made dull, for to this day the same veil remains when the old covenant is read. It has not been removed, because only in Christ is it taken away. Even to this day when Moses is read, a veil covers their hearts. But whenever anyone turns to the Lord, the veil is taken away. Now the Lord is the Spirit, and where the Spirit of the Lord is, there is freedom. And we, who with unveiled faces all reflect the Lord's glory, are being transformed into his likeness with ever-increasing glory, which comes from the Lord, who is the Spirit."

Let me show you some principles from this passage of Scripture that Paul documents for us. Some of the principles will be statements I make and others will be based on a questioning that will lead you to a proper understanding. (I do have a purpose for this exercise… please stick with me.)

1. When someone is not a believer in Jesus Christ (also referred to as being unsaved, not a follower of Jesus Christ, not a disciple of Jesus Christ, on "The Long Black Train" or on "The Highway to Hell") verse 15 says about them that "when Moses is read, a veil covers their hearts."

    Question – What is this reference to "Moses" by Paul?

    Answer – The answer is that Paul is referring to the books of the Bible in the Old Testament that Moses wrote. Those in the first century would have had access to these Old Testament books of Moses.

2. Question – What does a veil do?

Answer – It conceals, covers, hides or obscures something. In this case the unbelievers minds are being veiled (verse 14 says "made dull") to the true meaning of the Bible.

3.   Question – How does an unbeliever's veil become removed?

Answer – Verse 16 gives us the answer to this question… "when anyone turns to the Lord, the veil is taken away." This means that if you made the decision to pray, believing and confessing Jesus Christ as Lord and Savior, your spiritual "veil" has been taken away and you now have what verse 17 says is "freedom." This freedom comes from the unveiling that the Spirit of the Lord has caused to happen in your life (verse 17).

4.   Question – What does this spiritual unveiling by believing in Christ mean for you?

Answer – Previously, as being spiritually "veiled," the meaning of the Bible was concealed, covered, hidden or obscured to you. Now that you have been "unveiled," the Spirit of the Lord is free to disclose, reveal, show and teach you truths from the Bible that you were not previously able to see.

5.   Question – What is the ultimate purpose of the "unveiling" and "freedom" you now have upon receiving Jesus Christ as Lord and Savior?

Answer – The middle of verse 18 documents the ultimate purpose as "being transformed into his likeness with ever-increasing glory." As I mentioned in the opening paragraph, your decision to accept Jesus Christ is just the starting point. God's intention and plan for you is to become more and more like him (holy) every day.

It is with regard to the "being transformed into his likeness with ever-increasing glory" that we find in verse 18 that I want to devote the rest of this chapter. I believe that now that your spiritual "veil" has been lifted that there are some extremely important Biblical principles that you need to understand as it relates to your work ethic, work quality, responsibilities to your employer etc. This additional unveiling that I want the Spirit of the Lord to do for you in the Scriptures is what I'm going to take you through in the rest of this chapter. With each passage of Scripture that I have listed you will see some of my brief comments. I hope and pray that you will take these principles to heart in your everyday work.

Proverbs 18:9

"One who is slack in his work

is brother to one who destroys."

Point – Your employer has hired you to perform certain tasks, processes, jobs or responsibilities. Regardless of what your personal viewpoint of those tasks, processes, jobs or responsibilities are you need to perform them to the best of your ability, skill and strength. If your work ethic slacks off (becomes lazy or purposefully slow) you are taking resources, time and money away from your company because you are not being as productive as you could or should be. This slacking on the job, and resulting lack of productivity, has the effect of taking away from that company. This taking away can result in the destruction of the company if not corrected.

Proverbs 22:29

"Do you see a man skilled in his work?

He will serve before kings;

he will not serve before obscure men."

Point – Regardless of the tasks, processes, jobs or responsibilities you were hired to do, you need to become the most knowledgeable, productive, skilled person who has ever done them. I have seen time and time again where an associate that had a position that was deemed less glamorous than others took the job and did it with such excellence that they were promoted, advanced and awarded with more responsibility as well as more money and/or benefits. Keep in mind that the timeframe or schedule for promotion or advancement may not be as fast as you want it to be, but if you perform your job with excellence you will ultimately be rewarded.

Proverbs 12:11

"He who works his land will have abundant food,

but he who chases fantasies lacks judgment."

Proverbs 28:19

"He who works his land will have abundant food,

but the one who chases fantasies will have his fill of

poverty."

Point – The culture of the timeframe when this was written was highly agricultural so the "works his land" portion held a deep meaning for the readers in the era in which it was written. Today, many people are aligned with manufacturing, technology or service industries and not agriculture. However, the overarching principle of these two Proverbs pertains to "work" regardless of farming or whatever type work you are doing. The basic premise is that if you work you will have food but if you constantly chase after fantasies you are going to have difficulties with where your next meal is coming from. You need to be a committed worker and not someone who tries to sponge off others. Give your all to your employer and you will be blessed.

Ecclesiastes 5:18-20

"Then I realized that it is good and proper for a man to eat and drink, and to find satisfaction in his toilsome labor under the sun during the few days of life God has given him—for this is his lot. Moreover, when God gives any man wealth and possessions, and enables him to enjoy them, to accept his lot and be happy in his work—this is a gift of God. He seldom reflects on the days of his life, because God keeps him occupied with gladness of heart."

Point – The book of Ecclesiastes can be kind of confusing at times but there are some wonderful principles as it pertains to work. The point of the passage of Scripture listed above, and what I want you to take away from it, is that you should be the most joyful, glad, exuberant, excited, happy person in your workplace regardless of what job, task, process or responsibility you are assigned. This section of Scripture says we should be satisfied in our work (verse 18) and then says to be "happy in his work" (verse 19). Don't walk around all the time with a negative spirit…you should be the most positive person in your workplace regardless of the type of work you have been assigned.

Ecclesiastes 9:10

"Whatever your hand finds to do, do it with all your might, for in the grave, where you are going, there is neither working nor planning nor knowledge nor wisdom."

Point – The point of this is very simple…do your job, task, process or work with everything that you have (all your might). Don't hold back.

Colossians 3:22-25

"Slaves, obey your earthly masters in everything; and do it, not only when their eye is on you and to win their favor, but with sincerity of heart and reverence for the Lord. Whatever you do, work at it with all your heart, as working for the Lord, not for men, since you know that you will receive an inheritance from the Lord as a reward. It is the Lord Christ you are serving. Anyone who does wrong will be repaid for his wrong, and there is no favoritism."

Point – I understand that these verses are dealing with slavery. However, the type or condition of slavery that you are probably thinking about right now is not exactly the type of "slavery" being referred to here. Without getting into all the details of first century slavery, there is a work component principle that I need to share with you out of this passage. First of all let's look at the heart of this passage. The heart of the passage is found in verse 23…"Whatever you do, work at it with all your heart, as working for the Lord, not for men." If the writer is here instructing slaves to work with all their heart in spite of less than ideal conditions in slavery, how much more do you think that we as employees or associates that are compensated fully for our time should do our work as working for the Lord with all our heart? I want to challenge you to do your best

119

at everything, regardless of the situation you are in. Even if you don't think you are being treated fairly, justly, or equitably on the job, you do it with all your heart as unto the Lord. Verse 24 says that if you do this "you will receive an inheritance from the Lord as a reward."

The essence of this passage pertains to working with diligence. By the way, diligent is my favorite work word. Merriam-Webster's Collegiate Dictionary-Tenth Edition defines diligent as "characterized by steady, earnest, and energetic effort." And Merriam-Webster's Collegiate Thesaurus provides synonyms for diligent such as "industrious, persevering and persistent." I think you can see why diligent is my favorite work word….if you do your job, work, tasks, responsibilities and processes with diligence you will shine brightly in your workplace. To put an exclamation point on this chapter's teaching and principles I will close out with four Proverbs that deal with diligence. I will not provide any additional comments on these four Proverbs but rather let them sink in as you read them.

Proverbs 10:4

"Lazy hands make a man poor,

but diligent hands bring wealth."

Proverbs 12:24

"Diligent hands will rule,

but laziness ends in slave labor."

Proverbs 13:4

"The sluggard craves and gets nothing,

but the desires of the diligent are fully satisfied."

Proverbs 21:5

"The plans of the diligent lead to profit

as surely as haste leads to poverty."

Hopefully this book has done a twofold unveiling in your life. First, I hope the veil of workplace issues or temporary insanity has been lifted from your eyes and you now understand completely what your responsibilities are as it pertains to being an excellent, diligent worker and applicant. Secondly, I hope the spiritual veil has been lifted from your eyes and you have truly moved from the Kingdom of the devil to the Kingdom of God. I challenge you to reflect back over the principles and truths of this book as often as necessary to reinforce the importance of operating with excellence in every area of your life. This life is meant to be lived with zeal and passion not just simply as if you were punching in and out each day, just existing.

ALAN BALMER

Appendix 1:

Facebook Faux Pas Frenzy

Facebook post number 1

Interview tip #1- Friday I spoke @ a job fair & shared info about staffing services & interview tips. One tip was on attire…don't wear halter tops, spandex etc. Some rather large ladies have done this revealing their midriff when they really shouldn't. A colleague told me that they refer to that as coming in looking like a busted can of biscuits.

Facebook post number 2

Interview tip #2- When applying & interviewing, don't bring your Mommy with you. Worse yet, don't let your Mommy drag you in 2 get a job. Employers aren't interested how much your Mommy wants you to get a job, but how much YOU desire a job. You'd be surprised how often this happens. You should also not bring friends/family with you just to "hang out."

Facebook post number 3

Interview tip #3- Please bathe (for the love of all that is good & right) before going to interview.You would be amazed @ the amount of Lysol we go through in the office. Oh…& use deodorant, comb your hair & brush your teeth. Or if appropriate, comb your teeth and brush your hair.

Facebook post number 4

Interview tip #4- When applying/interviewing take your sunglasses off. You're not trying out for the music video for Timbuk3's "The Future's So Bright I Gotta Wear Shades." More interview tips to come.

Facebook post number 5

Interview tip #5- Upon coming to the office to apply/interview and discovering the mound of info we need and the length of time it will take to process, don't mumble "BS." It significantly reduces/ eliminates your chance to get a position.

Facebook post number 6

Interview tip #6- When coming to the office to interview, LEAVE YOUR CELL PHONE IN THE CAR!!!!!! There isn't much more annoying (except for intense body odor) than when an applicant answers his/her cell phone in the middle of an interview. It speaks volumes that you really don't care if you get a job or not. Guess what…you're probably not going to get the job. Also not appropriate…texting.

Facebook post number 7

Interview tip #7- If you call in to check on your status to be placed as a temp at a particular client of mine and I explain that you're not eligible and then while hanging up on me you drop the F bomb on me and my staff, it's probably not worth your time to call back 3 minutes later stating you are going to come see me with your "degree paperwork" because you are a diamond in the rough…diamond…no…rough…yes.

Facebook post number 8

Interview tip #8- When applying/interviewing, if we select you to continue with the process for a job you will be asked to give a urine specimen for a drug test. While in the drug test bathroom, don't ask one of my staff members to talk to you (because you like the way they talk) through the small window while you are filling your specimen cup. It weirds them out when you do that and you won't get the job.

Facebook post number 9

Interview tip #9- When applying/interviewing, it is not in your best interest to be covered from head to toe with glitter. Remember…all that glitters is not gold. Thanks to Lorena for this one…happened yesterday.

Facebook post number 10

Interview tip #10- If I have you placed on assignment at a client and you stop coming to work, don't follow call in procedure & then quit without notice, don't expect me to place you at another client even though you try to play a trump card that your VERY close relative holds a VERY high ranking position at the other client. Homey don't play that game!!!!! (Homey D. Clown/Damon Wayans…In Living Color)

Facebook post number 11

Interview tip #11- If you are going to falsify a DR excuse and turn it in for proof why you were absent from work, make it look real. Why? When we call that medical provider to verify it (because it looks phony) and they say they have no record of you as a patient, you will lose your job!!!

Facebook post number 12

Interview tip #12- If you ignore my phone messages for 2 weeks & at the end of 2 weeks I am actually able to make phone contact with you but you hang up on me, don't come back to me 3 months later begging for a job. I will tell you the truth when you beg…the truth is you will never be hired by the Company I work for. BTW, this person wouldn't have answered the phone if I hadn't called from my cell phone & tricked them.

Appendix 2:

Top ways of decreasing your chances of being selected for a job assignment at a staffing/ temporary agency

1. Not being truthful on an application or during an interview.

2. Not completely disclosing everything on an application.

3. Inappropriate dress or attire during an interview.

4. Attitude, rudeness, or arguing. Treat every person in the staffing/temporary agency with respect.

5. Trying out pick up lines on the staffing agency employees.

6. Using illegal drugs and then failing a drug screen (note…. if you are doing illegal drugs, don't waste your time or a prospective employers time).

7. Poor personal hygiene.

8. Scratching your private areas or putting your hands down your pants while interviewing.

9. Bringing someone with you to apply and interview.

10. Being late for your appointment to interview.

11. Poor handwriting that is hard to read.

12. Leaving gaps of employment on your application.

13. Calling in each and every day after you apply to check on your status. Follow the staffing/temporary agencies instructions on calling in to check for work.

14. Not being prepared to interview the same day you apply.

15. Using your cell phone during the application and interview process.

16. Not maintaining good eye contact or having inappropriate body language during the interview.

17. Speaking negatively about previous employers, supervisors or co-workers.

18. Only appearing concerned about money and benefits during the interview.

Appendix 3:

Random song titles from which I share work principles

Song: "40 Hour Week For a Living" (Alabama – 1985);
            "Working 9-5" (Dolly Parton – 1980)

Principle: Work all the scheduled work days that your
            employer requires. This will keep you out of
            attendance trouble.

Song: "Hard Workin' Man" (Brooks & Dunn – 1992)

Principle: Always put everything you have into your job. Do
            your job with excellence and diligence.

Song: "Hard Habit to Break" (Chicago – 1984)

Principle: Sometimes workers have habits that make them less than what their employer would consider the "Best" employee. Try to determine what your negative work habits are and break them.

Song: "Workin' For a Livin'" (Huey Lewis and the News – 1982)

Principle: 2 Thessalonians 3:10-12 "For even when we were with you, we gave you this rule: "If a man will not work, he shall not eat.""

Song: "Another One Bites the Dust" (Queen – 1980)

Principle: This is the song Human Resource professionals sing when someone quits or gets fired. Don't make your employer's Human Resources Professional sing this song by being a quitter or forcing their hand in terminating your employment.

Song: "Takin' Care of Business" (BTO – 1973)

Principle: If you will simply do what you are supposed to do, in the timeframe that you are supposed to do it (ie Takin' Care of Business) you will be okay.

Song: "Sweet Emotion" (Aerosmith – 1975)

Principle: Sometimes the emotions you display in the workplace aren't all that "sweet." You might want to consider how you come across to fellow workers, supervisors or subordinates.

Song: "Lyin' Eyes" (Eagles -1975)

Principle: 1) Tell the truth 2) Sometimes, when interviewing someone, the eyes tip me off if someone is lying or not. Luke 11:34, "Your eye is the lamp of your body. When your eyes are good, your whole body also is full of light. But when they are bad, your body also is full of darkness."

Song: "Bang Your Head" (Quiet Riot - 1982)

Principle: This is what Human Resources Professionals want to do when workers don't do what their supposed to do and it creates a "situation" that we have to investigate.

Song: "Lawyers, Guns, & Money" (Warren Zevon – 1978)

Principle: Once lawyers have to get involved in "situations" it becomes much more difficult, lengthy and costly to resolve.

Song: "Baby Don't Forget My Number" (Milli Vanilli
               - 1989)

Principle: Your employer more than likely has a policy or
               procedure for calling in when you are absent.
               Memorize that number and use it when you are
               going to be out of work or late.

Song: "As Soon As I Hang Up The Phone" (Loretta Lynn
               and Conway Twitty - 1974)

Principle: When speaking with someone on the phone, don't
               hang up in the middle of the conversation. Be
               courteous.

Song: "Call Me When You're Sober" (Evanescence -
               2006)

Principle: Don't show up to work under the influence of drugs
               or alcohol.

Song: "Take This Job And Shove It" (Johnny Paycheck -
               1977)

Principle: This is not the phrase to utter, say, scream, yell or
               holler when you are quitting. Make sure you follow
               your company's requirements for giving notice of
               your intent to quit. And please, don't just give the
               notice but actually work it out.

Song: "Who's Cheatin' Who" (Charly McClain – 1980)

Principle: Cheating has no place at the worksite (or anywhere else for that matter).

Song: "Dude Looks Like A Lady" (Aerosmith - 1987)

Principle: Be very careful what you call people in the workplace. Sometimes people aren't actually the gender you think they are.

ALAN BALMER

Appendix 4:

Items that will help you stay out of trouble on a job.

1. Immediately report workplace injuries to the designated person or persons at the business where you are working.

2. Observe all safety rules.

3. Comply with all policies and procedures.

4. Do not leave work early.

5. Do not return late from lunch or breaks.

6. Maintain production standards.

7. Maintain quality standards.

8. Work all they way up to the assigned shift end time (don't leave your workstation early).

9. Do not participate in horseplay or practical jokes.

10. Do not sleep on the job.

11. Do not use abusive, offensive, derogatory or threatening language.

12. Do not create an intimidating, hostile, or offensive working environment.

13. Do not fight with or attempt to injure other people.

14. Do not commit fraudulent acts.

15. Do not misrepresent, lie or falsify information, records, documents etc.

16. Do not steal from your employer.

17. Do not damage property.

18. Do not report to work under the influence of alcohol or drugs.

19. Do not possess alcohol or drugs while on the worksite.

20. Comply with legitimate instructions of management and supervision (the failure to do this is considered insubordination).

21. Do not interfere with the work of other workers.

22. Do not take company information outside of the company (ie comply with any confidentiality agreements or policies).

23. Do not use email, computers or other company owned property except for authorized company purposes.

24. Do not solicit during work time.

Appendix 5:

Random stories about applicants and associates

MJK…Years ago in Sylacauga when we first started doing drug screens, I sent an app into the BR with a small Styrofoam cup and drew a line at the bottom and advised not to go above that line…he didn't, but came out with # 2 in the cup…talking about throwing up!!!!!!

SB….I have a story for you- My story is from when we had paper applications and the applicant had to complete them. I had an applicant write the following reason as to why she was no longer employed at a particular site- "They turn nay me." It took me forever to figure out what she was saying until I annunciated it. (Alan's interjection…if you are still having trouble determining what "turn nay" means, it was an applicant's attempt at spelling "terminate.")

AB....I once had a temporary staff member that called in sick for the day. She said she was feeling terrible and would not be able to make it to work. However, later that morning she showed up to pick up her paycheck.

Appendix 6:

Teaching used to develop Chapter 17

KINGDOM (OF GOD) ENTRANCE QUESTIONS (These are listed to help you understand where the teaching is headed and what I want you to think about as you read through it.)

- What is the Kingdom of God?

- What is the message of the Kingdom of God?

- Why would we want to be in the Kingdom of God?

- How do we enter the Kingdom of God?

- What are some responsibilities after entrance into the Kingdom of God?

KINGDOM ENTRANCE OVERVIEW (these are 4 sections that will be covered in this teaching)

- Realizing the PROBLEM.

- Results of the PROBLEM.

- Resolving the PROBLEM.

- Responsibilities upon resolving the PROBLEM.

1. REALIZING THE PROBLEM (All Scriptures are from the NIV Bible.)

a. 1 Corinthians 6:9 "Do you not know that the *wicked* will not inherit the kingdom of God?" The Bible gives us a clear understanding of what *wickedness* is and defines it as *sin*.

b. Galatians 5:19-21 "The acts of the *sinful nature* are obvious: sexual immorality, impurity and debauchery; idolatry and witchcraft; hatred, discord, jealousy, fits of rage, selfish ambition, dissensions, factions and envy; drunkenness, orgies, and the like. I warn you, as I did before, that those who live like this will not inherit the kingdom of God."

c. Other verses to review on your own.

- Ephesians 5:3-5

- Matthew 15:19

- Exodus 20:1-17 (The Ten Commandments)

- It becomes clear that SIN is a *negative thing* in the Bible. SIN is the PROBLEM. Let's now come to an understanding of the results of SIN.

2. RESULTS OF THE PROBLEM

a. First of all let's establish the reach of sin and see who it impacts.

- Romans 3:23 "for *all* have sinned and fall short of the glory of God."

- 1 John 1:10 "If we claim we have not sinned, we make him out to be a liar and his word has no place in our lives."

- So who does the PROBLEM pertain to? Everyone; that includes me and you reading this book!!!!

b. Now that we understand the PROBLEM pertains to me and you and all humanity, we can see what the consequences of it are.

- Romans 6:23 "For the wages of sin is death......"

- Matthew 5:29-30 "If your right eye causes you to sin, gouge it out and throw it away. It is better for you to lose one part of your body than for your whole body to be thrown into *hell*. And if your right hand causes you to sin, cut it off and throw it away. It is better for you to lose one part of your body than for your whole body to go into *hell*."

- Revelation 20:12-15 "And I saw the dead, great and small, standing before the throne, and books were opened. Another book was opened, which is the book of life. The dead were *judged* according to what they had done as recorded in the books. The sea gave up the dead that were in it, and death and Hades gave up the dead that were in them, and each person was judged according to what he had done. Then death and Hades were thrown into the lake of fire. The lake of fire is the second *death*. If anyone's name was not found written in the book of life, he was thrown into the lake of fire."

3. RESOLVING THE PROBLEM

a. Now that we REALIZE the RESULTS of the PROBLEM, let's come to an understanding of how we can RESOLVE the PROBLEM.

- Romans 6:23 "For the wages of sin is death, but the gift of God is *eternal life* in Christ Jesus our Lord."

- Ephesians 2:8-9 "For it is by grace you have been saved, through *faith*—and this not from yourselves, it is the gift of God— not by works, so that no one can boast."

- 1 John 1:9 "If we *confess* our sins, he is faithful and just and will *forgive* us our sins and purify us from all unrighteousness."

- 2 Corinthians 7:10 "Godly sorrow brings repentance that leads to *salvation* and leaves no regret, but worldly sorrow brings death."

  b. Other verses to review on your own.

- 1 Peter 3:18

- Matthew 4:17

- Philippians 2:10-11

4. RESPONSIBILITIES POST PROBLEM

  a. Now that we understand how the PROBLEM can be RESOLVED, we need to understand what our RESPONSIBILITES are upon our personal resolution of the PROBLEM.

  b. Matthew 7:21-23 "Not everyone who says to me, 'Lord, Lord,' will enter the kingdom of heaven, but only he who does the *will* of my Father who is in heaven. Many will say to me on that day, 'Lord, Lord, did we not prophesy in your name and in your name drive out demons and perform many miracles?' Then I will tell them plainly, 'I never knew you. Away from me, you evildoers!' "

c. Romans 14:17-19 "For the kingdom of God is not a matter of eating and drinking, but of *righteousness, peace and joy* in the Holy Spirit, because anyone who serves Christ in this way is pleasing to God and approved by men. Let us therefore make every effort to do what leads to peace and to mutual edification."

d. 1 John 3:9-10 "No one who is born of God will continue to *sin*, because God's seed remains in him; he cannot go on sinning, because he has been born of God. This is how we know who the children of God are and who the children of the devil are: Anyone who does not do what is right is not a child of God; nor is anyone who does not love his brother."

e. Matthew 28:18-20 "Then Jesus came to them and said, "All authority in heaven and on earth has been given to me. Therefore go and *make disciples* of all nations, baptizing them in the name of the Father and of the Son and of the Holy Spirit, and teaching them to *obey* everything I have commanded you. And surely I am with you always, to the very end of the age."

<u>Review Questions</u>

■ What is the Kingdom of God? _____

_____

_____

_____

_____

■ What is the message of the Kingdom of God?

_____

_____

_____

_____

_____

■ Why would we want to be in the Kingdom of God?

_____

_____

_____

_____

_____

■ How do we enter the Kingdom of God?

_____

_____

_____

_____

_____

■ What are some responsibilities after entrance into the Kingdom of God?

_____

_____

_____

_____

_____

**Intermedia
Publishing Group**

Publishing That Works For You

Do you need a speaker?

Do you want Alan Balmer to speak to your group or event? Then contact Larry Davis at: **(623) 337-8710** or email: **ldavis@intermediapr.com** or use the contact form at: **www.intermediapr.com**.

Whether you want to purchase bulk copies of *Temporary Insanity* or buy another book for a friend, get it now at: **www.imprbooks.com**.

If you have a book that you would like to publish, contact Terry Whalin, Publisher, at Intermedia Publishing Group, (623) 337-8710 or email: twhalin@intermediapub. com or use the contact form at: www.intermediapub.com.